NEIL YOUNG

Carole Dufrechou

New York   London

Copyright © Quick Fox, 1978

All rights reserved.
Printed in the United States of America.

No part of this book may be reproduced or transmitted in any form or by any means, electronic or mechanical, including photocopying, without permission in writing from the publisher: Quick Fox, A Division of Music Sales Corporation, 33 West 60th Street, New York 10023.

In Great Britain:
   Book Sales Ltd., 78 Newman Street, London W1, England

In Canada:
   Gage Trade Publishing,
   P.O. Box 5000, 164 Commander Blvd.,
   Agincourt, Ontario M1S 3C7, Canada

In Japan:
   Music Sales Corporation,
   4-26-22 Jingumae, Shibuya-Ku,
   Tokyo 150, Japan

International Standard Book Number:
   0-8256-3917-4
Library of Congress Catalog Card
   Number: 77-088754

Designed by Jon Goodchild
Typeset by The Type Shop, California

Front cover photography by Andrew Kent/Mirage
Back cover photograph by Larry Hulst
Title page photography by Neal Preston/Mirage

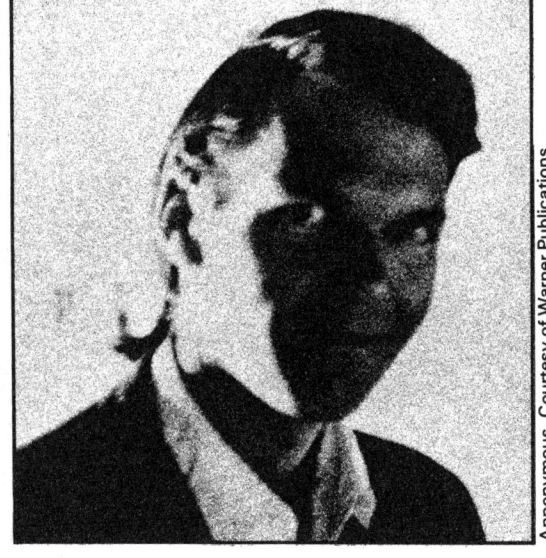

Annonymous. Courtesy of Warner Publications

Jim Marshall. 1966

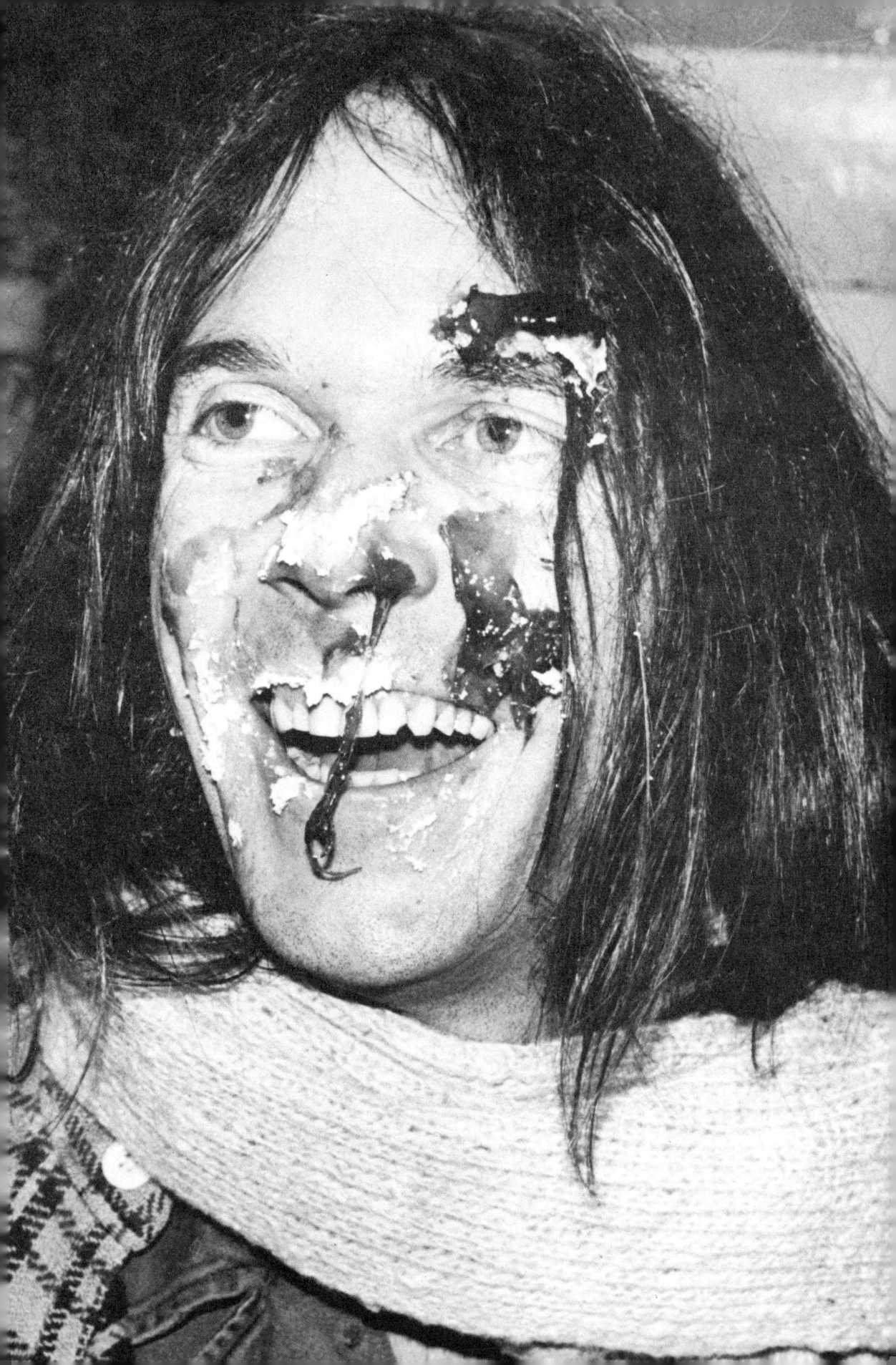

He has a shy and retiring personality, yet can arouse as much passion as anyone in rock today. He is intensely, uncompromisingly personal—extraordinarily aware of what moves, pleases, and hurts him—yet he's able to communicate in a vivid, driving language that moves audiences to near hysteria. His high, quivering voice has been called unusual, strange, and unique; once you are under its spell, it opens your mind and enlists your total attention. He comes on like a stoned-out, California hippie type, yet in reality doesn't "come on" at all.

He is a complex, sensitive, vulnerable artist whose duality is reflected in his performances and recordings. They can range from the gentle, almost balladlike soft-rock songs he plays with acoustic guitar to the pounding electric guitar solos that have driven audiences wild.

He is Neil Young, recently hailed by *New York Times* music critic John Rockwell as being "about as talented and touching a poet as American popular music has produced." Poet, singer, songwriter, guitarist, filmmaker, performer, Neil Young is one of *the* voices of rock 'n roll in the seventies.

In April of 1970, at age 24, he told *Rolling Stone* interviewer Elliot Blinder that he'd already been playing guitar for 9 years and didn't know how much longer he could do it. This interview, one of the few that Young has ever granted, took place during a period when he was reaching a peak in popularity. He was touring at the time with both the Crosby, Stills, Nash & Young group, and with Crazy Horse, whom he referred to as "my rock 'n roll band." He had recently released his solo album, *Neil Young*; the album *Everybody Knows This Is Nowhere*, backed by Crazy Horse; and had teamed up with Crosby, Stills and Nash to produce the extraordinary *Déjà Vu* album, released the same month that the interview appeared in *Rolling Stone*.

For Neil Young, it was like leading many different lives at once. The tours with Crosby, Stills and Nash were very successful. "It's blowing my mind," he told Blinder. "A lot of the applause, a lot of the reaction and everything. I don't know how it got so big—I knew it was gonna be big and everything because when I joined them they had a lot of hype out and everything. They had a good album out, you know, and they had a rapport there . . . so I mean I knew they were gonna be pretty big but I didn't think it was gonna be as big as this. It's big. Makes a lot of money and it's hard to relate to after what I was doin' before."

What he was doing before may not have been as big as what he suddenly found himself doing in the spring of 1970, but it is now a major chapter in rock record history. Early in 1965, Young, along with Stephen Stills and Richie Furay, formed a group in Los Angeles called the Buffalo Springfield. The group lasted until 1968 and released three albums: *Buffalo*

Susannah Aceveda

Jasper Dailey. Buffalo Springfield recording, 1966

Springfield, Buffalo Springfield Again, and the posthumous *Last Time Around.* Real commercial success eluded them during their short lifespan, but they still enjoy a near-legendary status, due in part to the fact that they carved some of the first trails through the new culture of the mid-sixties and in part to the superstardom reached by Neil Young.

Neil Young deserves his status as a superstar. He has produced 9 solo albums in his 13-year recording career, and in the fall of 1977 released his retrospective tenth, the 3-record LP, *Decade. His* words, *his* music, and *his* playing have made each album so successful and so extraordinarily timely. But that final ingredient—the sound of his voice—has catapulted him into his position of fame. "It's a quality of anguish mixed with probing clarity," according to *The Stars and Superstars of Rock,* "which, linked to the poetic simplicity of the best of his lyrics, has made him one of the most important performers around today."

Richard McCaffree. 1977

Although he seems to be the quintessential California, Neil Young actually was born in Toronto, Canada on November 12, 1945. The son of a noted sports journalist, Scott Young, Neil was raised in Canada's grain-belt region, Winnipeg, after his parents' divorce. His family, including younger brother Bob, still lives in Canada. Like everyone in his age group, Neil Young was greatly influenced by the fifties music that was crossing the border from the United States. While in his teens, Young taught himself to play guitar, imitating the rock music sounds of the day, particularly those of his favorite, Elvis Presley, and formed his first group, the folk-rock-oriented Neil Young and the Squires. The sixties folk music scene saw Neil Young and the Squires playing the coffeehouse circuit and they became a favorite among Winnipeg teens.

They didn't play together too long, though, for soon Neil was on his own, working the Canadian and border club circuit as a solo folk singer. It was during his travels in the mid-sixties that he met Stephen Stills in Canada. In 1965 he drove cross-country in his 1953 Pontiac hearse hoping to meet up again with Stills in Los Angeles.

He originally had intended to make it in L.A. as a folk singer and composer, but couldn't pass up a unique opportunity that came his way soon after his arrival. Stills had just arrived in Los Angeles from New York. In New York, Stills had sung and written arrangements for a 10-voice group, the Au Go Go Singers, who included Richie Furay. Stills' meeting with Neil Young had reinforced his idea of playing folk music with electric guitars. Once in L.A., all three came together to form a new group, The Buffalo Springfield, along with Bruce Palmer on bass and Dewey Martin (formerly of The Dillards) on drums.

In a very insightful article on Neil Young in *Cue* magazine of February 1971, James Lichtenberg had strong words of praise for Buffalo Springfield. "Along with Dylan, Jefferson Airplane, and The Byrds, Buffalo Springfield was one of the earliest, finest American groups.... Buffalo Springfield—the combination of Indian with Lincolnesque Gothic America is quite

Jim Marshall. 1966

apt—appeared . . . as a five-member group from Los Angeles, whose two dominant figures were remarkably contrasted. Steve Stills, the blond, direct, energetic leader, wrote half the songs on their first album, *Buffalo Springfield*, with self-assured titles like 'Pay the Price,' 'Leave,' and 'Everybody's Wrong.' Neil Young, deep and dark, wrote the rest of the songs with reflective titles like 'Out of My Mind,' 'Burned,' and 'Flying on the Ground Is Wrong.' And even in the first album, there is evidence of a strange tug of war: Stills versus Young.

"Under the influence of Dylan and The Beatles, new-culture music was was blooming with positive statements. In contrast to the rest of the Springfield—and Stills in particular—who were generally imbued with this mood, Young had a startling way of being uncertain [as you can tell in the lyrics to 'Do I Have to Come Right Out and Say It?' and 'Mr. Soul'] . . . .

"*Buffalo Springfield Again*, their second album, was a fantastic, original departure, and ought to have done for the Springfield what *Rubber Soul* did for The Beatles: elevate them far out of simple rock and roll as major voices in new culture. Young's contributions were brilliant. . . . *Buffalo Springfield Again* should have been the event of the season. It wasn't. It was as if some tribal curse dissipated the energy of the group, in spite of the fact that by this time they had fanatic admirers, split into Young vs. Stills camps.

"*Last Time Around*, their final album, amid bitter weeping from the faithful, caused hardly a ripple among young audiences off to the far-out world of early psychedelic rock. . . . And that was that. Young fans blamed Stills. Stills fans blamed Young. But no one could change the bitter paradox that this most promising of American rock groups—like jazz groups of previous decades who awoke the morning after their break-up to find they were voted the finest—seemed gone forever."

They were gone forever as a group as of May 5, 1968. But their music will be with us for a long, long time.

The Buffalo Springfield were literally overnight successes. Also called the Herd, they received instant recognition from music insiders. One of their more amazing accomplishments is that before even one single record of theirs had been released they were featured in a concert at the Hollywood Bowl (July 25, 1966). One of the producers of "Hollywood Palace," an ABC TV show, saw them perform, became aware of the intense reception the group was receiving, and immediately signed them for 6 guest dates. Others in the record world also picked up on the excitement and popularity growing around the group. They were making a 7-city concert tour with The Byrds and performing regularly at the famous Whiskey-A-Go-Go on Sunset Strip. It's no wonder, then, that they were approached with contracts by over 20 recording firms. They signed with Atco Records, a subsidiary of Atlantic Records, mainly because of good vibes between Steve

Stills and Atco producers Charles Greene and Brian Stone. Shortly after the Hollywood Bowl performance, Stills' "For What It's Worth" made the Buffalo Springfield a nationwide hit, rising to Number 7 as a chart single in the U.S. in early 1967.

The Springfield climbed the usually long and tortuous route to fame in a short period of time; however, each member of that group had paid his dues. Musically, they were ready: each had been in preparation for just such an event for a very long time.

Neil Young had been involved in one way or the other with local rock 'n roll groups, usually as a guitarist, from the ninth grade on. He was so

involved with his music that he quit school before completing his secondary education. All he wanted to do was concentrate on singing, songwriting, and playing the guitar.

If you listen carefully to the lyrics of "Don't Be Denied," a song written in the early 1970s and recorded on his *Time Fades Away* album in 1973, you hear just how difficult his youth must have been, how much music and dreams of being a star meant to him. He sings about his father's leaving home: *"When I was a young boy/My mama said to me/'Your daddy's leavin' home today / I think he's gone to stay.'"* This is the period when he moved to Winnipeg, to face a new life with new schools, new friends and their new rules. *"When we got to Winnipeg / I checked in to school / I wore white bucks on my feet / When I learned the golden rule."* The golden rule obviously was "No Strange Apparel" (like white buckskin shoes, possibly worn in imitation of his favorite rock 'n roll star, Elvis), because *"The punches came fast and hard / Lying on my back in the school yard."* The refrain was: *"Don't be denied. Don't be denied."*

Not to be denied, Neil continued in his dream world of music and stardom: *"Well pretty soon I met a friend. / He played guitar / We used to sit on the steps at school / And dream of being stars."* Neil and his friend started a band, which put an end to their taking school work seriously. *"We started a band / We played all night. / Don't be denied, Don't be denied."*

After disbanding his Winnipeg group, Neil Young and the Squires, to strike out on his own, Neil made a record in Detroit with another group, The Mynah Birds. Bass-playing country-man Bruce Palmer was also a member of the Mynah Birds, and when the group's leader got drafted, Young and Palmer decided to head for the West Coast. Upon arriving in Los Angeles in 1965, Neil immediately set out to form a new group. After little initial success with getting a group of his own going, Neil, in company with Bruce Palmer, ran into Steve Stills, and the three immediately agreed to begin playing together. Lacking a musician's union card—lacking even United States working papers—Canadian Neil Young began working with his newly formed group and continued to work illegally during practically the whole Buffalo Springfield period.

Steve Stills, the other major force in the Buffalo Springfield, was born in Dallas, Texas on January 3, 1945. His Southern roots are very strong because his entire youth was spent in the South, except for two years spent in Illinois from age 4 to 6. He moved around with his family quite frequently. By the time he was 14, he had also lived in Houston, Texas; Covington, Louisiana; Gainesville, Florida; and Tampa, Florida. The latter part of his teens were spent in the Republic of Panama and in Costa Rica, where he was graduated from high school in 1963.

Besides being a singer, Stills is a versatile instrumentalist adept at guitar, keyboards, drums, and tambourine. His musical training included church music in Illinois and Louisiana, piano lessons in Gainesville, Florida, and playing along with his father's jazz records on his first drum set in 1955. Throughout high school and into college, Stills played trap drums and snare drums and occasionally directed the school marching band. He also played electric guitar in high school bands, including a stint with a local Florida group, The Radars.

For a short period of time, Stills was a political science major at the University of Florida in Gainesville, but he quit in 1963 and headed for New Orleans. He spent the winter of 1963 there, playing folk music on Royal Street; in 1964 he made his way to New York City. There he was introduced to folk-rock music and the 12-string guitar. During his few years in New York, he performed with various groups. One of them, The Au Go Go Singers, was a 10-voice vocal group for whom he sang and wrote lyrics. One of the members of the Au Go Go Singers who later played an important role in Stills' and Young's lives was singer and rhythm guitarist Richie Furay.

Furay was born in Dayton, Ohio on May 9, 1944. He grew up in Ohio and, while attending Otterbein College in Westerville, formed a folk trio. They were such a local hit that he also headed for New York to try his luck. Things went slowly for Richie at first, until he joined up with The Au Go Go Singers. This group cut one record, made a television appearance, and went on a concert tour. Before winding up in Texas in 1964, the group's tour took them through Winnipeg, where Furay and Stills met Young. The

Au Go Go Singers and Neil Young and the Squires played together for one performance. For Furay, Stills, and Young, things were never to be the same again.

With the 1964 split-up of The Au Go Go Singers, Stills headed for Los Angeles and Furay returned to New York. For the next year and a half, Stills and Furay lived hand-to-mouth existences on opposite coasts. During this time, Stills unsuccessfully tried to form a band with Van Dyke Parks, and even failed at an attempt to link up with the Monkees. When he met Neil and Bruce Palmer, Steve called Richie from New York to ask him to become the fourth member of their new group. They lacked only a drummer.

All four turned to Dewey Martin, a Canadian-born singer-drummer with a strong Southern tradition from his many years in Nashville, Tennessee. In the early 1960s, while in Nashville, Martin's drumming was recognized as being so good that he had played with the Grand Ole Opry, Patsy Cline, Carl Perkins, Faron Young, and Roy Orbison. The oldest member of The Springfield, Martin was born September 30, 1942, in Chesterville, Ontario, Canada. While on a visit to Los Angeles in 1964, he fell in love with the city and made plans to head out West. For a while he played as a sideman at recording sessions, then formed his own group, Sir Walter Raleigh and the Coupons, and moved to Seattle, Washington. He stayed there only a short time, though, for by the end of 1965 he was permanently back in Los Angeles. He had been playing with the bluegrass group The Dillards and was with a group called The MFO when Stills, Young, Palmer, and Furay invited him to join them. By March of 1966, Martin was hooked up with a group that people were still referring to as the Herd, but which came to be known once and for all as The Buffalo Springfield.

These five very strong-willed, individualistic, multitalented people merged into a single unit that is still being talked about ten years after its demise. They each contributed excellent musicianship, and their backgrounds and abilities enabled them to produce everything from folk music and country rock to hard rock. In *The Rolling Stone Illustrated History of Rock and Roll* (Random House, 1976), writers Miller and Kingsbury concluded: "While not really a folk-rock band, the prodigiously talented Buffalo Springfield deserve special mention both for caring enough to preserve the very best qualities of the form and for conscientiously consolidating them into inspired, if idiosyncratic rock and roll. Like the Byrds, the Buffalo could either hang back on a song until all of its somber juices boiled over ('For What It's Worth') or just come right out and say it ('Sit Down, I Think I Love You'). Although the group had a short but troubled career, their melodies, not their maladies, linger on in 'Mr. Soul,' 'Bluebird,' 'Broken

Arrow,' 'I Am a Child' and 'Kind Woman.'"

None of the album sales for Buffalo Springfield actually exceeded 200,000 copies, with the exception of *Retrospective*, released in 1969, which sold 400,000 copies over a 3-year period and made the top of the charts. In 1967 and 1968, the group had several chart hit singles besides "For What It's Worth," including Stills' "Bluebird," and "Rock 'n Roll Woman," and Young's "Expecting to Fly" and "On the Way Home."

Rejected album cover design, 1968

Their first album, *Buffalo Springfield*, was released in February 1967. All of the songs were written by either Stills or Young and set the pattern for the remarkable Springfield sound of strong melody and poignant words with up to four vocal parts playing against an acoustic backing—their own unique blend of rock and country music.

With the release of the second album, *Buffalo Springfield Again*, in December 1967, a number of personnel changes had taken place. Bruce Palmer was busted and deported to Canada after playing on half the album; he was replaced by singer-bassist Jim Messina. The album includes all originals by Stills and Young, as well as three songs by Richie Furay. Each composer produced his own songs and each track contained a credit telling who produced it and which musicians played on it.

At its peak in 1967, the Buffalo Springfield was being praised from all quarters and was often compared to The Beatles and The Rolling Stones. The music world was also looking forward to more great things from this phenomenal group. But internal conflicts abounded. Besides hassles among themselves, the group was also exhausted from their concentrated outpouring of records and concerts in such a short period of time. And then there were the run-ins with the police. On March 20, Neil Young and Richie Furay were busted along with Jim Messina and Eric Clapton of Cream, charged with possession of marijuana.

By the time of the release of their final album, *Last Time Around*, in August 1968, all the original members of the group had gone their separate ways; the group simply ceased to exist. *Last Time Around* includes five songs by Stills, two by Furay, and one by Messina. It is obvious that Neil Young had already gone on to other interests, as evidenced by his lack of musical contribution. There are only two songs by him on this last album. (They happen to be the best two).

In "On the Way Home," there's no mistaking the message coming across. It is one of the most expressive tunes of the late 1960s. When Young sings *"When the dream came, I held my breath with my eyes closed. / I went insane, like a smoke ring day when the wind blows,"* any listener who ever got stoned can again hear, feel, and recall every sensation associated with the act. *I Am a Child* was a joy. *Rolling Stone*'s Barry Gifford took it very lightly in his review of the *Last Time Around* album. He saw it as being in Tim Hardin's electric country-folk vein, with Young sounding exactly like Hardin. Gifford felt it was "a nice tune, very pretty, with some strikingly poignant lines: *'You can't conceive of the pleasure in my smile.'* It's very simple and light." Most would agree. *"You hold my hand, rough up my hair, / It's lots of fun to have you there,"* sings Neil. He's just singing about some of the simpler pleasures in life.

Gifford's highest praise was for the album. "As a final testament to their multitalents, the Buffalo Springfield have released *Last Time Around*, the most beautiful record they've ever made. . . . They sound, as Jim Messina croons, like a 'carefree country day'." Gifford's conclusion sums up the general feeling about the split: "Too bad it isn't the *first* time around."

On the album *Retrospective/The Best of Buffalo Springfield* released in January of 1969, the cream definitely rises to the top, for it contains the very best in music and lyrics the group produced. Young's brilliant "Mr. Soul" and "Broken Arrow," both from *Buffalo Springfield Again*, were two major works included in *Retrospective*.

"Mr. Soul" was viewed very differently by two different reviewers. One

saw it as "driving rock uniquely built on uncertainty" (*Cue*), and the other as a "gutsy contemporary blues" song that "hangs together well" (*Rolling Stone*). It is rock, it is blues, it is contemporary, and it is most definitely timeless poetry as well, with a meter, rhythm, and rhyme to it that stamp "Mr. Soul" as a classic for all times.

Read the first two lines: "*Oh, hello, Mister Soul, I dropped by to pick up a reason/For the thought that I caught that my head is the event of the season.*" Listen to the music just once. And you'll realize that the lyrics and music have become permanent sounds in your head, easy and enjoyable to play over and over again. Then try on the second verse. *"I was down on a frown when the messenger brought me a letter. / I was raised by the praise of a fan who said I upset her. / Any girl in the world could have easily known me better. / She said, 'You're strange, but don't change;' and I let her."*

"Broken Arrow" also a classic, is much more a reflection of the times in which it was written and is less universal than "Mr. Soul." It is long—over six minutes—and somewhat in the vein of a Beatles-type "freak out." Written when Neil was living in Hollywood, it's a reflection of what it's like to be a rock 'n roll star. "I was a Hollywood Indian," he told Elliot Blinder. "Everybody thought I was an Indian. That was when it was cool to be an

Indian. I was wearin' fringe jackets and everything. I really loved these fringe jackets . . . I dug wearing them."

There are many changes that take place in the song, including rhythm and mood, and the instrumentation ranges from beautiful, full-string orchestration to simple piano tracks. It opens with fans screaming in the background and Young rasping out a rendition of "Mr. Soul." The beat slows down, and it moves into a different song entirely. And the song/poem itself changes, each stanza offering a different message.

The first stanza deals with the pitfalls of fame, the woes and nightmares of being a star: *"The lights turned on and the curtain fell down, / And when it was over it felt like a dream, / They stood at the stage door and begged for a scream."* . . .

The second stanza, more oblique, deals with the discovery: "Eighteen years of American dream" is an illusion. And the panic at this insight: *"He hung up his eye lids and ran down the hall."*

In the final verse, the stately and royal images of a queen, a king, and a black-covered caisson seem to refer to the Kennedy assassination. *"The Queen wore the white of the county of song, / The black covered caisson her horses had drawn / Protected her King from the sun rays of dawn. / They married for peace and were gone."*

Shattered dreams, eyes opened wide to reveal illusions for what they really are, reality an *"empty quivered, brown skinned Indian on the banks that were crowded and narrow,"* holding a broken arrow. An unmistakable reflection of the times—1967. Neil thought so highly of both these songs that he included them on his *Decade* album. About "Broken Arrow" he tells us: "I wrote this after quitting the group in '67 due to one of many identity crises. Joined up again soon enough to cut this one though. Took over 100 takes to get it."

Even with the amazing amount of talent packed into The Buffalo Springfield, Neil Young's powerfully inventive figure rose to the top. He was singled out for national attention not only for his sparkling lead guitar work, but also for his well-known songs. He was reaching out and grabbing hold of listeners with the raw, vulnerable sound of his voice. His unmistakable, high-pitched, quivering vocals stamped him as a true original from the very beginning of his recording and performing career.

Out on His Own

Let's look at the period of quiet between The Buffalo Springfield's split in May 1968 and the return to the limelight of every member of the Springfield less than a year later. What was happening in the Los Angeles pop music scene can be summarized in two words—Country and Western. L.A. was then *the* music recording scene, so naturally the top C & W stars were drawn to it. The very top country stars in 1968 included Glen Campbell, Buck Owens, Merle Haggard, Roger Miller, Tex Williams, the Everly Brothers, and Johnny Cash. They all had recorded in Los Angeles during 1968. Country radio stations, country music clubs, and country music publishers were going strong. The Academy of Country and Western Music, an influential and prestigious organization, was located in L.A. Amidst the usual Hollywood glamor and glitter, C & W—or, the Nashville sound, rockabilly and country-rock as it was also called—had made itself quite at home.

Lovely Topanga Canyon, located only 20 miles from the heart of the bustling L.A. music scene, might as well be 2,000. Dusty and woodsy, it leads from Malibu in the south up to a sprawling suburban area in the north. It is a well-known area where many music people try to lead private and spacious lives. There Neil Young spent his initial period of seclusion after the break-up of the Springfield and before the release of his first solo album.

The other four members of the by-then-defunct Buffalo Springfield went on to join other groups. Before forming Crosby, Stills & Nash, Steve Stills cut the *Supersession* jam album with Al Kooper and Mike Bloomfield, played guitar on girlfriend Judy Collins' album, *Who Knows Where the Time Goes?*, and played bass on Joni Mitchell's first album. It is rumored that during this period Stills took guitar lessons from Jimi Hendrix.

It was at Joni Mitchell's Laurel Canyon home that Stills and Californian David Crosby (of the folk-rock pioneering Byrds) met and sang with Englishman Graham Nash, who was in town playing with the successful British vocal group, The Hollies. The three men never looked back. In December 1968, they announced their team-up after the trade deals were made. Nash was released from his Columbia contract to go with Atlantic. Stills already was under contract to Atlantic and Crosby was free at the time. David Geffen left Ashley Famous Agency to manage the new group, who began recording almost immediately for Ahmet Ertegun.

Their first album, *Crosby, Stills & Nash*, was released in 1969 and sold over two million copies in one year. It contains Stills' epic-length "Suite: Judy Blue Eyes," written for Judy Collins, which was also the group's first U. S. hit, as well as such masterworks as "Wooden Ships," "Long Time Gone," and "Lady of the Island." The group immediately received "supergroup" status for this largely acoustic LP filled with close harmonies. Even though no one would describe them as a country-and-western group, a country sound could definitely be heard and the album became an instant surprise classic.

Two other former Springfield members, Jim Messina and Richie Furay, formed a new group called Poco, which also received lots of good attention and praise, especially after their performances at the Troubadour in Los Angeles and the Fillmore in San Francisco. Poco had a definite country sound, as well as a highly successful commercial one. They retained much of the country-blues vocal sound that had made the Buffalo Springfield so popular, as well as their tight rock 'n roll rhythm. Furay wrote practically all the group's material and played rhythm guitar. Messina produced the records, played rhythm guitar, semi-lead, and some additional backup voice. Other members of Poco included Rusty Young on pedal-steel guitar and voice, Randy Meisner on bass and voice, and George Grantham on drums.

Meanwhile, the fifth member, Dewey Martin, tried getting three new members together to keep the Springfield name going. He quickly realized it just wasn't going to be the same and returned to session work.

When Neil emerged from seclusion in January 1969, it was to release his first solo LP, *Neil Young*. Among the notables playing with Young on the album were Jack Nitzsche and pedal-steel guitarist Ry Cooder. The album did not get raves, either from reviewers or from Young's fans. But is is a very strong, good first album because, above all, the message comes out loud and clear: This is me, Neil Young, this is who I am.

Like an actor, one of Neil's strengths is to get his listening audience completely involved from the very first line of dialogue. This uncanny dramatic ability is obvious from the first vocals on Side One of the first album: *"He's the perfect stranger like a cross of himself and a fox. . . ./Know when you see him, nothing can free him./Step aside, open wide, it's the loner."*

"The Loner" may very well reflect Neil's mood of isolation after the breakup of what he probably had hoped would be an ideal, ongoing, always-growing musical brotherhood. He was living at the time on David Briggs' couch in Topanga Canyon. Although he was able to get himself together very quickly to produce *Neil Young*, considering the upheaval he'd just been through, some of the bitterness and disillusionment Neil felt is evident in the lyrics: *"If you see him in the subway, he'll be down at the end of the car, / Watching you move until he knows he knows who you are."*

About the breakup of The Buffalo Springfield, Neil told *Rolling Stone* on August 30, 1970: "A lot of changes went down in everybody's heads when the group broke up. When we got together we thought we were gonna be together about fifteen years. We really thought it was gonna last a long time because we knew how good it was. Nobody else did, though."

Other comments on *Neil Young* noted the album's strengths. "Especially vivid is Young's sense of melancholy and the ingenious clusters of images he employs in his lyrics," wrote Gary von Tersch in his *Rolling Stone* review of *Neil Young*. "'The Loner' is a contemporary lament that features a nice blending of Neil's guitar with strings in non-obtrusive fashion, allowing Young's balanced ice-pick vocal to chip effectively at the listener."

"Ice-pick vocal," an apt image for the sound of Neil's voice on the record. "When I was with the Springfield, I held back vocally," Neil told an interviewer a few months after his first album was released. "I was paranoid about my voice. So on my own first LP, I buried my voice intentionally." He buried it perhaps, but couldn't keep it down, couldn't prevent it from coming out and stabbing at his listeners, demanding that they pay attention to every word he had to say. The passion, the intensity were there, and they seemed to peak in the last song on the album, "The Last Trip to Tulsa."

Very different from the rest of the album, which maintains many Springfield-like qualities, "Last Trip" is Dylanesque. On this 9-minute cut, there is only Neil's chameleon voice and his guitar work, without any strings, piano, or drums. It is a strong, prsonal drama that builds from verse to verse and becomes more abandoned as it goes along. It seems layered with many meanings at once: the early stirrings of the ecology movement; the fear of being overrun by society, mechanization, and indifference; and the feminists' fight to stop everyone from dividing personality traits like aggressive and sensitive into masculine and feminine.

Even though lots of people dug "Last Trip to Tulsa" more than anything else on the album, Neil Young didn't like it. "After the album came out that's the one I really didn't like, and I still don't," he told *Rolling Stone's* Elliot Blinder. "It sounds overdone. It just sounds like it's a mistake to me, and luckily it's cool."

"Here We Are in the Years" also heralds what was to become in the seventies a major world movement—ecology. Neil urges us to "*Go to the country, take the dog,/Look at the sky without the smog,/See the world, laugh at the farmers feeding hogs, eat hot dogs.*" It's a return-to-nature plea, a desire to get back to the basic human qualities he could see we were rapidly drifting away from: "*While people planning trips to stars/Allow another boulevard to claim a quiet country lane,/It's insane.*" This song is introduced by Jack Nitzsche's instrumental piece entitled "String Quartet from Whiskey Boot Hill." "It is a slow, deliberate, ethereal introduction to Neil's vocal on 'Here We Are in the Years,'" wrote Gary von Tersch in *Rolling Stone*. "Musically the piece is string-dominated and very lush and full with Neil's voice incising between—the scraping fade-out says it all." Von Tersch is referring to the last line: "*Lives become careers, children cry in fear, 'Let us out of here!'*"

A different sort of song from "Here We Are in the Years" is "If I Could Have Her Tonight." Here we find Neil's unique ability to express another human quality we can all relate to—uncertainty: "*Oh if she came to me, would she be kind?/And if she stayed with me, do you think that she'd like to do/Anything I would, or would she leave me?*" It's performed with slow, crystal-clear ease. "It features a heavy drum line, Byrds-like guitar and mellow lyrics that all together add up to that unique sense of melancholy yet joy in melancholy which the Springfield captured so well," wrote von Tersch.

"I've Been Waiting for You" is along the same lines as "If I Could Have Her Tonight," but with organ and piano accompaniment. It's short and succinct and again includes that element of romantic uncertainty: "*I've been looking for a woman to save my life,/Not to beg or borrow,/A woman with the feeling of losing once or twice,/Who knows how it could be tomorrow?*"

Rick Griffin

SHOP Nº 0003
Neil Young and Crazy Horse

In May 1969, less than five months after *Neil Young* was released, Neil came out with his second solo album, *Everybody Knows This Is Nowhere*. It was backed by a group called Crazy Horse. When asked by Blinder how he came to be with Crazy Horse, Neil answered in his usual rambling style: "I met all of them during the first six months that I was in L.A., when The Buffalo Springfield was just getting together, and they didn't know how to play at that time, not very well . . . they were just hangin' out, and I was starting to work with the Springfield, and I met Jack Nitzsche shortly after that and then he joined . . . they were called the Rockets."

The Rockets were actually a well-established group on the West Coast made up of Danny Whitten on vocals and guitar, Ralph Molina on drums, and Billy Talbot on bass. With the addition of producer-arranger-songwriter Jack Nitzsche, the new group, Crazy Horse, was complete.

Crazy Horse and Neil had only been together for eight weeks when they cut *Everybody Knows This Is Nowhere* and had been together only six or seven days when the now-classic "Down by the River" was cut.

Neil could have waited until they were better meshed, as many other stars would have done. After all, it was an important album for Young. His first had been only moderately successful; to establish himself as a solo artist, a lot hinged on this second album. But impatience, pure guts or drive made Neil record his second album quickly. There was a quality there between himself and his new backup group that he wanted to catch before it was dissipated in long, drawn-out practice sessions and rehearsals. "There is something on those records that was recorded . . . like it was when we were really feeling each other out, you know, and we didn't know each other, but we were turned on to what was happening. So I wanted to record that, because that never gets recorded. And that's just what that album is, it's just the bare beginnings," Neil noted (*Rolling Stone*, April 30, 1970).

What a beginning! With his second LP, Neil gave more voice to the recordings, more confidence. Crazy Horse gave him more confidence and security—and it is obvious throughout the album. "A calmer, sunnier person, having proven himself with his first solo album, Young . . . brought forth a work of soaring California rock, rich in electrical guitars and peaceful vibrations as in the most popular cut from the album, 'Cinnamon Girl,'" one reviewer commented (*Cue*, February 13, 1971).

In "Cinnamon Girl," we do indeed find a sunny, happy Neil Young, feeling very positive about what he wants! *"I want to live with a Cinnamon Girl, / I could be happy the rest of my life with a Cinnamon Girl."* The poetic images reflect his mood: *"A dreamer of pictures, I run in the night / You see us together, chasin' the moonlight, my Cinnamon Girl."* He included this song on *Decade* with this cryptic note: "Wrote this for a city girl on peeling pavement coming at me thru Phil Ochs' eyes playing finger cymbals. It was hard to explain to my wife."

"Cinnamon Girl" was one of Neil's favorites from this album, along with "Everybody Knows This Is Nowhere" and "Round and Round and Round." These three songs achieved a special musical quality of togetherness and immediacy that Young was striving consciously for. He had a feeling for, and understanding of, the records made in the fifties and sixties. They stood out as *right* to him, because they were recorded all at once. And Neil wanted to make records of that same quality. "The singer is into the song and the musicians were playing with the singer and it was an entity, you know," he told Elliot Blinder. "It was something special that used to hit me all the time, that all these people were thinking the same thing, and they're all playing at the same time."

This quality is apparent in "Round and Round and Round" because it was done all in one session, not dubbed and overdubbed during different sessions. The acoustic live thing bores some people, but others find this the most appealing part of the album. "Round and Round and Round" is a song that must be listened to attentively—preferably with earphones on—in order to get into the sound and rhythm of it. Written rather early in his career (c. 1967), "Round and Round and Round" weaves a spell. There is a waltzlike quality to the song, in its steady repetition of sound and melody. If you imagine yourself twirling to the music, a spinning sensation comes on you as though you're caught in a dizzying web of cotton candy. It's like moving lazily but steadily in circles under brilliant chandeliers around a glittering grand ballroom. *"Round and round and round we spin, / To weave a wall to hem us in, It won't be long, it won't be long."* And then, *"How slow and slow and slow it goes, / To mend the tear.*

In "Everybody Knows This Is Nowhere," the title song from the album, Neil sang about L.A. With the hectic pace he was maintaining during this period, he felt a strong need to just get away from it all, to get out of the center of the whirlwind that the L.A. recording scene had him caught up in. His frustration at the impossibility of escaping, and his bewilderment can be heard in the song. Neil had a strong need to "go back home and take it easy," although he was doing what so many others would have given their right arm to be doing ("*Everybody seems to wonder what it's like down here*"). People may wonder what it is like and wish that they also were there creating, but for Neil, with his strong needs for country, peace, and solitude with the lady he loved, L.A. was nowhere right then. "*There's a woman that I'd*

like to get to know livin' there . . . / I gotta get away from this day-to-day runnin' around, / Everybody knows this is nowhere."

"Down by the River" (c. 1967) is a harsher song than any other on the album and one of the longest (over 9 minutes), with considerable guitar work inbetween chorus and verse. It's almost like a crying against what Neil envisions in the bend of the road as the seventies come into view: "*You take my hand, I'll take your hand, / Together we may get away / This much madness is too much sorrow, / It's impossible to make it today.*"

"(When You're on) The Losing End" is the most country-and-western song on the album. There is great pickin' on acoustic guitar with a genuine, steady country beat throughout. It opens Side Two and is completely different from anything else on the record. Even the lyrics are country, with their storytelling tale of woe, as if the singer is taking you into his confidence about his broken heart. He sings about going into town to find his girlfriend but she's not at home. So he talks to some friends, then he wanders off alone. He tells us how hard it is for him now, but that somehow he will make it, even though he'll just never again be the same. Then, as though he's having an imaginary conversation with the girl he can't find and letting us listen in on his musings, he sings: *"Won't you ever change your ways, / It's so hard to make love pay when you're on the losing end, / And I feel that way again."* He tells his girlfriend that he misses her more than ever and that since she's gone he can barely make it. *"Things are different round here ev'ry night, my tears fall down like rain"*—a true C & W lament. You can't help but suffer with him as you listen to the miserable state he is in. At the same time, you can't stop your foot from tapping to the terrific country beat.

To *Rolling Stone* reviewer Bruce Miroff, the most interesting tracks on this second album were "Running Dry" and "Cowgirl in the Sand," the last two on Side Two. In *Running Dry*, there is also a lament for a lost love, but this time it is done in a folk style, almost like a medieval minstrel melody: *"I left my love with ribbons on and water in her eyes. / I took from her the love I'd won and turned it to the sky."*

"Building on a traditional folk melody," wrote Miroff, "'Running Dry' interweaves electric guitar and violin into a disquieting blend. Its aura of strangeness is somewhat reminiscent of Young's magnificent 'Out of My Mind.' The lyrics are a bit over-dramatic, but the music and vocal manage to transcend them, creating the feeling of a dimly understood tragedy." Most would agree with this insight into *Running Dry*, especially after listening carefully to the chorus: *"I'm sorry for the things I've done, / I've shamed myself with lies, / But soon these things are overcome and can't be recognized."*

For Miroff, every element in "Cowgirl in the Sand" worked perfectly. "The lyrics are quietly accusative while the lead guitar, alternately soaring, piercing, and driving, keeps the song surging forward": *"Hello, Cowgirl in the sand. / Is this place at your command? Can I stay here for a while? / Can I see your sweet, sweet smile? / Old enough, now, to change your name. / When so many love you, is it the same?"*

In this song, the vulnerable Neil Young emerges, struggling with his susceptibility to romantic bondage. "At the outset of his career in 1968, after leaving Buffalo Springfield, Young seemed to revel in his own passivity, to enjoy the complete abdication of personal responsibility," *The Rolling Stone Illustrated Encyclopedia of Rock and Roll* observed, and continued: "If the lilting melodies and careful rhymes of his early work made him attractive, the emotional stance rendered him even more so. Just as [Laura] Nyro's following seemed principally composed of women, Young struck a responsive chord in many men; his simultaneous abandonment to love and yearning for revenge against that promiscuous Cowgirl in the Sand held a cryptic promise of release. (Unlike Mitchell, Nyro or Cohen, Young never chose to rage against his own vulnerability, although he did know full well how to complain about it; that naive blamelessness made him inviting, too.)"

Neil later revealed that he wrote "Cowgirl" on the same day that he wrote "Down by the River." He was lying in bed sweating, with scraps of paper covering the bed. He was running 103°. That could bring out the romantic in many of us! The real key to the success of "Cowgirl in the Sad," however, according to Miroff, was Neil's singing. The song "demonstrates quite clearly the peculiar depths of Young's voice," Miroff concluded.

It's always back to the same thing—Neil's voice—with its "peculiar depth" and its "high-pitched intensity." It is a voice unlike any other singing rock 'n roll. Nobody would call it an excellent, even a good voice. But then, rock 'n roll singers in general don't have what would classically be considered good voices. What they have are unusual voices, voices that are forces in themselves, reflecting the unique temperament of the singers and the songs they sing. Dylan and Jagger, for example, have voices that sometimes grate and scrape harshly across a song. Yet they are insistent voices, never letting the listener go once he is taken in their grasp. Neil's voice is that way. It can be high. It can be low. It can moan or shriek out a ballad or hard rock song. It can lull you and rock you, or jar your senses so hard you're forced to sit up and hang on to every word he says. "While Neil Young is a good songwriter and an excellent guitarist, his greatest strength is his voice," wrote Miroff. "Its arid tone is perpetually mournful, without being maudlin or pathetic. It hints at a world in which worry underlies everything." And because most of us recognize that world and have been a part of it, Neil's singing moves us intensely. "In a natural and moving way, Neil Young is the Johnny Ray of rock and roll."

With the emergence on his second solo album of Neil's voice, his fame was insured. He had a newfound confidence in himself as a singer that the listeners could feel as well as hear. His rise to the top of the rock 'n roll world naturally gained momentum as more and more listeners got hooked on Neil Young's unique sound.

Everybody Knows This Is Nowhere was a huge success. In fact, it was one of the smash successes of 1969-1970. It moved onto the charts in November 1969 and remained there until mid-1971, earning Neil and Crazy Horse a gold record. Less than a year after its release, audiences would be rocked by Neil Young again. This time he would be playing with a completely different group on an album that would come to embody the feelings of an entire generation of young people.

SHOP № 0004
Young Joins Crosby, Stills & Nash

"It all started one late summer afternoon in a picturesque house in Laurel Canyon. Crosby was preparing material for a solo album after having left the Byrds. Nash, still with the Hollies, was visiting, and Stills, after the breakup of the Buffalo Springfield, had been sitting around and staring at the side of a mountain trying to decide what to do next in between playing sessions. Goofing around in the California living room, they all began to play and sing together. And they loved it immediately and they talked about making an album and boy, it was going to be a hassle with each of them contracted to a different record company. Music-biz wunderkind David Geffen, a 26-year-old funky imp, was called in to move minds and signatures around to make it possible, no small feat, mind you, but he did and then some." That's how Ellen Sander (*Hit Parader*, September 1969) described the beginnings of Crosby, Stills & Nash. This all took place in the summer of 1968; by early 1969 their first album, *Crosby, Stills, & Nash*, had been released to instant acclaim as one of the best of the year. Later it was voted Number One for 1969 by many major polls and it won a gold record, remaining on the charts into 1970.

But for all the acclaim, the three felt that something was missing—something vital that they needed in order to produce the true sound they were striving for. And that something turned out to be Neil Young—the final ingredient that made their particular mixture of melodies complete.

In April 1970, Neil had this to say to *Rolling Stone*'s Elliot Blinder about why the three had asked him to join them:

"The reason that they asked me to join in the first place is 'cause they couldn't tour just as Crosby, Stills and Nash, 'cause they haven't gotten anybody to play the instruments." (But what about Dallas Taylor and Greg Reeves who played with C S & N? asked Blinder.) "Well, yeah, bass and drums," responded Neil. "So what have you got? Bass and drums, rhythm guitar and Stephen. It's not enough for that big sound. They want more.

Jim Marshall. Big Sur Folk Festival, 1969

Few guitars, organ at the same time as piano, they wanted a big group, I guess."

When asked how they went about getting Neil to join them, Neil responded: "Steve came over to the house one day and asked me to join. First they didn't want to be called Crosby, Stills, Nash and Young. They just wanted it to be Crosby, Stills and Nash. They said, 'Everybody'll know who you are, man, don't worry about that.'"

Obviously everything straightened out, for by August 1969 they were officially called Crosby, Stills, Nash and Young, once jokingly referred to as

Courtesy Atlantic Records

"the best-sounding law firm in pop." They were to record on Atlantic, which posed no problem for Neil, because his label, Reprise, and Atlantic were both part of Warner Brothers.

Neil joined the group on the same loose basis on which the others had originally agreed. Each one wanted to be completely free to work with other groups or as an individual. Neil had no intention of abandoning his solo career and insisted he would also continue to perform and record with other musicians whenever he could.

Graham Nash felt the same as Neil and was actually speaking for all of them when he told Ellen Sander: "It's important that you don't talk about us as a group, because we're not. We're individuals and we're making an album together. If it comes off, so we're all proud of it. But it's not a group.... I don't want to feel as if I have to be in a certain place at a certain time, to arrange my life to suit anyone but me. If you're in something groovy and something groovier comes along, well, you should go and do that."

They never intended C S N & Y to be a band that required their full-

time energies and commitment, which is probably why they were able to produce only one studio album together, *Déjà Vu*. Released in March 1970, it was *Billboard*'s number-one album of the year and had orders totaling $2 million before it even reached the stores.

What were the factors in making *Déjà Vu* such a phenomenal success? It immediately followed a very active performing period in 1969, the same year the group appeared at Woodstock, sang Joni Mitchell's song of the same name, and appeared in the movie, which recorded that staggering event on film.

Another reason for the success of *Déjà Vu*, Neil thought—and the main reason he was so proud of the album—was that all five songs he played in were recorded in the studio with no overdubbing and with everyone playing and singing together all at once. This was especially true of "Helpless" and "Country Girl." Both were pure, spontaneous and instantaneous. According to Neil, David Crosby agreed that this was the right way to make records. "David likes to do it that way too," Neil told Blinder, "because he likes to get off, he really likes to get off. So one of David's songs, 'Almost Cut My Hair' . . . it's really Crosby at what I think is his best. It's like all live, three guitars, bass, organ and drums and it's all live and there are no overdubs, one vocal and the vocal was sung live."

While just about every reviewer heaped praises on *Déjà Vu*, *Rolling Stone*'s Langdon Winner was far from enthusiastic. "Along with many other people," he wrote, "I had hoped that the addition of Neil Young to Crosby, Stills and Nash would give their music the guts and substance which the first album lacked. Live performances of the group suggested that this had happened. Young's voice, guitar, compositions and stage presence added elements of darkness and mystery to songs which had previously dripped a kind of saccharine sweetness. Unfortunately, little of this influence carried over into the recording sessions for *Déjà Vu*. Despite Young's formidable job on many of the cuts, the basic sound hasn't changed a whit. It's still too sweet, too soothing, too perfect, and too good to be true." Winner said that Side Two was a showcase of the foursome's strong points—"precision playing, glittering harmonies, a relaxed but forceful rhythm, and impeccable twelve-string guitars." However, he thought the songs just weren't first rate. To Winner, even "Country Girl," which continued in Neil's tradition of massive production numbers, fell short when compared to some of his earlier work.

Cue's James Lichtenberg didn't have very many kind words to say about *Déjà Vu*, or about the four together as a group, for that matter. To him, Neil was simply allowing himself a sentimental side-trip by linking up again with Steve Stills to create "what was billed in advance as the super-group of the decade." Because of the unresolved individual talents in the group and the atmosphere of their always being on the verge of a breakup, Lichtenberg considered *Déjà Vu* a "frantically hyped anthology of unrelated music." He noted that Neil managed to rise above any failings the group had as a whole, however: "The others have suffered musical loss, but Young seems impervious, creating in concert and on record his own untouchable universe. His two songs on *Déjà Vu* are so purely individualistic that the amorphous quality of the group slides away like water off the proverbial duck."

The Stars and Superstars of Rock gave the following reasons for the album's success: "*Déjà Vu*, like a very few albums before it, seemed for a moment to focus the feelings of every young American who went out and bought it.... Here were songs of hope for the new lifestyle, like Joni Mitchell's 'Woodstock' and Nash's 'Our House,' and balanced against them the powerful sadness of Young's 'Helpless' and Stills' '4 & 20.' And in a weird way David Crosby's 'Almost Cut My Hair' seemed to sum up the confusions and paranoia of living in Nixon's America."

The Woodstock Nation

When Crosby, Stills, Nash & Young faced an audience of 500,000 at Bethel, near Woodstock, New York, in the summer of 1969, they were only a part of the largest collection of rock 'n roll talent ever assembled at one time in one place. Joan Baez; Blood, Sweat and Tears; Richie Havens; and dozens of other stars better known to the crowd performed over that long, rainy, 3-day weekend. But by the following summer, C S N & Y were pulling larger crowds and making more money than almost any other performer or group who had played at Woodstock. Somehow they had struck at the very heart of the generation with their music, lyrics, and personalities. That day in 1969, facing an enormous crowd of people, a link was formed between the group and the audience when they burst forth with honest awe: "Hey man, I just gotta say

that you people have gotta be the strongest bunch of people I ever saw. Three days, man! Three days! We just love you, we just love you . . . . This is our second gig. This is the second time we've ever played in front of people, man! We're scared shitless!"

With that kind of spontaneity, and with the songs they sang that wound up on *Déjà Vu,* C S N & Y managed to capture the mood and spirit of the entire nation. Only in their twenties at the time, each had, however, accumulated over a decade of musical experience. They had already earned the recognition and respect of their colleagues as the highly skilled musicians and songwriters; soon the larger crowds were to offer them recognition also.

Stills and Young were the main writers for the group and also carried major star status since both were already household names. Crosby and Nash also had been major forces in the music scene before joining the group and were especially noted for their harmonies.

David Crosby, a native Californian, was born in Los Angeles on August 14, 1941. His musical beginnings were with a New-Christy-Minstrels-type group, Les Baxter's Balladeers, and as a solo folk singer. Then he met and joined up with Roger McGuinn and Gene Clark, all three forming the center of The Byrds (previously also known as The Jet Set and The Beefeaters). Crosby contributed some of the best songs The Byrds ever recorded, as well as a wide musical scope and vision. But egos, among other things, eventually caused a rift. Most people agreed that Crosby was trying on a new image, a new life-style, and that it just didn't fit the more conservative Byrds. For example, his song "Triad" (about a *ménage à trois*— *"Why can't we go on as three?"*), was too risqué for The Byrds and they wouldn't even record it. The Jefferson Airplane wound up making it very popular on their *Crown of Creation* album, and later Crosby got to record it on *4 Way Street*. He was also getting politically heavy (for example, in songs like "Long Time Gone" and "Almost Cut My Hair."). Again, this went against The Byrds' image and was later much better suited to Crosby, Stills, Nash and Young.

Handsome Graham Nash was born in 1942 in Blackpool, England, and grew up in Manchester. While still in grammar school, he and his good friend Allan Clarke formed a group called The Two Teens. They played together quite a lot and in 1963 they formed The Hollies. For a long time in the sixties, The Hollies consistently made the charts and were second only to The Beatles in hit singles in Britain. Nash was unquestionably the leader of The Hollies, writing their songs and singing, as well as playing rhythm guitar. In the late sixties, he wanted to change the group from its simplistic pop style to the more aware sounds coming out of the California "flower power" period. The group didn't want to change, however, and Nash found himself hanging out more and more frequently with Stills and Crosby in California. That fateful summer afternoon described earlier, when the three first played and sang together at Joni Mitchell's house, is now part of rock music history.

The addition of Greg Reeves and Dallas Taylor actually brought the group up to six. Gregory Reeves, like Steve Stills, plays many instruments. He studied drums, tambourine, clarinet, and violin when young, then began playing bass when he was 15. A quiet guy and the youngest of them all

(only 19 when he joined the group), Greg came to them straight from Motown's studios.

Dallas Taylor was born in Denver, Colorado, in 1949. He grew up in San Antonio, Texas and moved to California in 1967. He and John Sebastian were good friends, and it was through John that he met Steve Stills. He became the drummer for The Buffalo Springfield and then played on the original *Crosby, Stills & Nash* album.

Their sound now complete, the six members of C S N & Y hit the road as performers. This was the era of supergroups and super-performances, and while many others were better controlled and more tightly organized, there was a quality about C S N & Y's live act that was enormously pleasing and satisfying to the crowds. They took chances on stage that other groups would have been petrified to take. Probably because they were so loosely organized as a band in contract, the looseness carried over into their concerts. Often it was aggravating, since audiences wound up waiting for each member, particularly Young, to tune up to perfection. But once underway, they were unbeatable. Their relationships as individuals and as musicians charged them to real highs in their performances.

Their debut in Los Angeles was an exceptional success in every way. They were a sellout all seven nights at that city's fashionable Greek Theater, even though the people who usually went there were used to acts like Johnny Mathis and Henry Mancini and, as one promoter put it, they were "not used to seeing quite that much hair on men!" But opening night ended any earlier worries. As the same promoter told *Rolling Stone* on October 4, 1969: "At the box office it was incredible. [The kids] came out of the hills in trucks ... we had to turn hundreds away."

A pattern for their live performances was established immediately. They played an acoustical first half, bringing on the electric guitars, drums, and bass for the second half. Joni Mitchell preceded them at the Greek Theater; that evening's concert was to a large extent folk music. The group earned standing ovations and encores practically every night that week.

A few months later, they performed again at the Winterland Auditorium in San Francisco. In between rehearsals and performances, all four talked to *Rolling Stone*'s Ben Fong-Torres. He wrote a lengthy article about them in the December 27, 1969 issue of *Rolling Stone*, concentrating on where they felt they were at that particular time in their lives, both personally and musically.

The Women in Their Lives

At the time of the Fong-Torres interview, Neil already had been married for a year. He had met his wife, Susan, in 1968 at a Topanga Canyon cafe she was running at the time. As Fong-Torres described her, she was a "lovely girl with sweet Judy Collins eyes." Their only plan was to remain in Neil's hillside Topanga Canyon redwood house where they had been living since August 1968. Neil had even begun building a 16-track recording studio under the house. Both his home life and professional life were progressing well during this period. If he were to make any changes at all, it would be to move either to Big Sur or back to Canada.

Dallas Taylor also was married at the time, but the others were going through some heavy women-changes. "We've canceled a lot of studio time because of woman troubles," Nash told Fong-Torres matter-of-factly. "Women are the most important thing in the world, next to music."

David Crosby only recently "had been spun nearly out of his mind" when his lady of nearly three years, Christine, was killed in a bus collision on a road near his Novato home. To escape, and to work out his pain, David sailed a schooner for a while; then he and Graham spent time in England to unwind. When he returned, he threw himself into his work, keeping up a happy front even with his friends, still trying to ease his loss, although he never tried to suppress the wonderful memories he had. "Man, you know how hard it is to find a good woman, a woman who's just right—who's with you on every single level. Every step of the way it was right. But you know, at least you know that it *can* happen," he told Fong-Torres. Steve Stills had lost Judy Collins, Graham had recently parted from Joni Mitchell, and Greg Reeves was in a slump over his girlfriend.

Their Music

Graham Nash talked about why the six were performing together as a group. "We didn't have a *band* with just the three of us. We could sing the LP, but we couldn't play it." For their concerts, he noted: "We knew we'd have to represent the sound we had on the album [which included overdubs of additional guitar tracks.] Now we have a whole different band."

A whole different band because of Neil Young, primarily. In the studios, according to Stills: "We may shape the album ["we" meaning himself, Nash, and Crosby], but Neil will come along and give us that extra thing." Nash agreed with this: "He gives us that bit of direction we may need to resolve a question. He's good at making records." And Stills went even further, calling Neil "another life force." He said "I always wanted another rhythm section. But instead of a keyboard man, we thought, why not a guy who could do other things—write songs, play guitar, be a brother and stuff."

"In the studios," wrote Fong-Torres, "Neil, who so often clashed with Stills in the illuminating but frustrating Springfield days, stands back, generally. His scowling, black-topped demeanor, big-eyed, glowering stares shining out between messy curtains of hair, makes him a natural for solitude, and he seems content in the shadows, thrashing his guitar mercilessly, like a country bluesman possessed. Young is a satisfied man—secure with his own band, Crazy Horse, on Reprise Records, as well as this insane, perfect gig with this superb, if not 'super,' group."

Although Stills had been the leader of Buffalo Springfield, Young had been the most outstanding. "Tallest, darkest, fringiest, writer of some of their best songs . . . and he was the most desultory and uppity, quitting the band twice before they folded, saying he never wanted to be in a group anyway just like you wouldn't have Dick Nixon to kick around anymore," Fong-Torres noted. How different Neil Young was from Steve Stills. "In the studios, Stills is a man of restrained excitement, of quiet pride, of nonstop devotion to the task of making records," Fong-Torres observed. Young said of his opposite: "Steve's whole thing right now is the group. It'd be impossible to have everybody into it as much as him. It'd be complete bedlam."

Fong-Torres described Crosby and Nash during this period as "cheerleaders." At recording sessions, they would be "conducting playback parties for visitors and heaping mountains of praise onto their colleagues." Crosby was in heaven: "This is the best music I've made with other people," he beamed. When Nash talked about their recording and playing, he emphasized the feelings and moods of the group. "Our main thing is to set some kind of a mood; our only rule when it comes to choosing our music is to pick something that gets us off."

As the sixties were nearing an end, C S N & Y as individuals and as a group had only loose plans. Besides juggling his life and schedule to meet the demands of touring and recording with two groups, Neil considered it very important to have his own private life, filled with different interests that would give him a chance to express himself creatively in a variety of ways. He was beginning to get into the movies and filmmaking. He wrote a song for the movie *Strawberry Statement*. With Crazy Horse as musicians, he was doing the score for *Landlord*, which he described as a "racial comedy."

He had just bought a Beaulieux Super 8, which was only the first step in filmmaking for him. He told Fong-Torres, in his tongue-in-cheek manner, that he and Susan then planned to hit the "big time." They would blow up to 16mm the scored films they had made on their Super 8, then show them at the Topanga Community House—the same place the local women's club usually met!

Crosby and Stills were settling into Marin County. David already had a ranch in Novato, in north Marin, and Steve was looking for a house. Greg lived about 90 miles north of San Francisco. In spirit and in locale, San Francisco and environs was the place to be for all of them, the place that provided the life-style and working conditions best suited for their sound. It was also the place for other music groups, including The Jefferson Airplane and The Grateful Dead. Jerry Garcia hung around them so much that he became an unofficial member of the group, dropping in on recording sessions and playing pedal steel guitar.

"They Can Do No Wrong"

This was C S N & Y's most intense period musically, and for Neil it was like being turned on 24 hours a day. He had commitments to two very different groups and had to work out schedules so that he could tour with each and give to each the very different kinds of creative music it required. And he was making plans to record another solo album. He was very concerned that he might lose Crazy Horse, or that they would just dissolve. "I didn't want Crazy Horse to die just as we were getting it together," he said. While C S N & Y provided him with tight, structured music, Crazy Horse was "funkier, simpler, more down to the roots," with lots more bass and drums. The technically well-advanced side of Neil was fully satisfied with C S N & Y; the looser, more down-to-earth side performed best with Crazy Horse. "They complement each other inside me," he noted.

With Crazy Horse, Neil was always the lead singer and had complete production control. With C S N & Y, Neil sang lead only on his own numbers, the others backing his high, hard-edged, quivering voice with waves of their own specially blended smooth harmony. Neil did very little harmony singing to back the others; it just wasn't his style. "The main thing with that group is their singing, the three of them singing, and they sing those three-part harmony things and occasionally I sing a fourth part, but not often," he told Blinder (*Rolling Stone*, April 1970). "It's the same sort of general role I played in Buffalo Springfield: I play lead guitar and occasionally I'll sing a song, and I'm quite happy to do that as long as I can do my own thing, because my songs actually require a different kind of thing than that anyway, so I'm quite happy to do them with Crazy Horse. We do most

of them, they're just different. I couldn't do *Everybody Knows This Is Nowhere* with Crosby, Stills and Nash."

After the *Déjà Vu* album and much touring, Neil was best able to assess what was happening in his life on all these different levels—and just how this life-style was affecting him—in his interview with Elliot Blinder. He ws asked if he lead the kind of life where he was busy every day with more than one thing! Obviously, every day was a juggling act. "Yeah, it's like living two different lives," Neil responded. "People who see me and come over and want to talk to me because of Crosby, Stills and Nash are weird compared to the people I know through Crazy Horse; and then there's the people I know who don't have anything to do with either of them, who are a whole other trip, and by the time the day's over I'm just completely screwed up. I start off real well depending on which one I see first. . . . It's getting to be a lot of work. It's getting to be no privacy at all."

Neil took his commitments to both groups very seriously and worked hard not to short-change either one. Even though he just might have finished a strenuous tour, gone home to record an album, and set out on the road for 30 to 40 days for another tour, he felt he couldn't say no when asked to play again right on the heels of all this nonstop activity. He explained to Blinder: "Crosby, Stills and Nash have been resting for two or three months, right; they're ready to go back on the road, so it's hard for me to say 'Let's not go on the road now, let's wait, because I've been on the road playing with Crazy Horse.' That just doesn't seem like a very good reason to them."

Both groups brought Neil a lot of pleasure during this time, each in its own way. When talking about playing with Crosby, Stills & Nash, Neil said: "The music is good, the music is exciting to me, it's more pop than Crazy Horse. Crazy Horse is liable to have a bad night, you know, and I think Crosby, Stills and Nash just isn't liable to have a bad night because the personalities are there. If the music isn't happening that night, just the fact that those three guys are there makes it cool. You know if you see Clapton having a bad night, you're still seeing Clapton . . . and that's the way the kids feel, there's still that other trip happening . . . . But with Crazy Horse, nobody knows who they are really, nobody's familiar with them except for maybe Jack [Nitzsche], and now when we go out to play . . . we're used to playing at home, playing in the studio."

The studio he is referring to is the one he had completed by this time underneath his home in Topanga Canyon. Along with a P.A. system and good walls, it had all the equipment anyone could need. "It's really groovy," Neil continued, "and we play in there, and that's where we get sound . . . and like we don't play together very much, 'cause there's no time . . . we're about as loose as you can get."

Neil's great warmth and affection for the guys in Crazy Horse came across clearly when he talked about them. "They're really down, I don't know if you can tell by lookin' at 'em, but they're not your usual bunch of rock and roll guys . . . they're just not that way," he told Blinder. "They're very funky, I think they're great. I don't know if you have to live with them to know how great they are or what. I don't know if the people are really hearing what I hear, you know."

Backed by Crazy Horse, Neil's concert tour during the early part of 1970 was successful. As an individual performer, Neil seemed to finally be getting the kind of recognition he had deserved ever since his frustrating days with Buffalo Springfield, and which he lacked even as a member of C S N & Y. John Morthland, in a review of one of Neil's performances

during this tour, wrote glowingly in *Rolling Stone* (April 30, 1970). "Everything about Neil Young's approach to music has become so highly personalized that when he performs, he seems at first to be oblivious to his audience. That impression is a superficial one, though, for his music demands rapt attention, and he quickly establishes such an intimate relationship to the audience that even a college gym seems like a cozy little club . . . . Like a Crosby, Stills, Nash and Young concert, a Neil Young concert begins with an acoustic set. Neil plays acoustic in a hard, percussive manner, while still keeping intact his captivating melodies."

And when Crazy Horse joined the rest of the set, the concert got even better. "Crazy Horse is a strong band that gives Young all the support he needs," Morthland stated. When they did "Down by the River"—the song the crowd had been waiting for and the one they knew the best—"Young displayed amazing virtuosity. Pacing the stage in his patched blue jeans, his head jerking up and down with the music, he picked guitar lines seemingly out of nowhere, piling them up one staccato note on top of another, never once letting you forget those lyrics, 'I shot my baby!'"

Neil even managed to charm the audience in between songs, telling them stories about near-accidents the group was always having and giving his amusing observations on grass. But Neil's lyrics and, of course, his extraordinary voice, were what most impressed Morthland: "Part of Young's power rests in his imagery, which, while sometimes strange, is almost always rich and evocative. Another asset is his high quivering voice which is also unique. He seems most at ease with Crazy Horse, and they in turn fit his style better than any of the other bands he's worked with. On this night *they could do no wrong* anyhow, and, on leaving the gym, I noticed that most everyone was going home happy. It's easy to see why."

Morthland felt Young and Crazy Horse were the best combination and "could do no wrong"; Fong-Torres had exactly the same thing to say about Young with Crosby, Stills and Nash. "At this point," he had written in December of 1969, "*they can do no wrong*. It could be the flawless harmony—tight as the Everly Brothers'; soft as Simon's and Garfunkel's; melodic as the best of the Springfield. It could be reports, word-of-mouth about the mini-Woodstocks they'd created wherever they performed, sending out those effortless good vibes and coming off like 'gentle free spirits.' It could well be a mass appreciation of their aversion the kind of hype that flooded Blind Faith, making them an instantly high-priced, out-of-reach act."

It could have been all those things, plus the fact that they were four controversial characters, each with his own opinions, each with his own strong statements and style, as Neil had pointed out. Whatever it was, Fong-Torres noted (December 27, 1969): "Crosby, Stills, Nash and Young are coasting. Their next album [their soon-to-be-released *Déjà Vu*] is pre-sold gold [an accurate prediction], judging by their success across all fields of music—Top 40, 'underground' and 'middle of the road' (their LP *Crosby, Stills & Nash* even reached Number 35 on *Billboard*'s Soul Survey). Their concerts are near-perfect, the group relaxed in subdued light, making love with their soft, bluesy, acoustic music, slapping palms, soul style, after a particularly pleasing number, then charging on with a full load of amps and speakers, then collapsing in a circular embrace at the end of it all."

The group continued touring throughout 1970 and 1971, its popularity growing with each performance. In April of 1971 they released their only other group album *4 Way Street,* which was made up of music recorded live during a number of different concerts. Reports were constantly circulating about their breaking up. In May of 1970 there was a sudden spurt in productivity. They came out with their hit single "Ohio," and began another tour with a new drummer, Johnny Barbata, a powerful drummer who had played with The Turtles before joining C S N & Y, and a new bassist, Calvin Samuels, who took Greg Reeves' place on bass when Greg was let go immediately before the May 1970 tour.

"Ohio" took everyone by surprise, including Crosby, Stills, Nash, and even Young himself. "Neil surprised everybody," Crosby is reported saying in *Rolling Stone* of June 25, 1970. "It wasn't like he set out as a project to write a protest song. It's just what came out of having Huntley-Brinkley for breakfast. I mean we've all stopped even watching the TV news, but you read headlines on the papers going by on the streets." Young told Crosby: "I don't know; never wrote anything like this before . . . but there it is. . . ." "Ohio" appears on their album *4 Way Street* and later on Neil Young's *Journey Through the Past* and *Decade.*

Written in the aftermath of the Kent State killings, "Ohio" seemed to sum up the shock and horror the entire country was feeling in Neil's lyrics: *"Tin soldiers and Nixon's coming/We're finally on our own/This summer I hear the drumming/Four dead in Ohio."* And the song asked questions hundreds would agonize over: *"What if you knew her and/Found her dead on the ground/How can you run when you know."*

A timely song, definitely, but timeless in its own way as well. Ironically, seven years later, in September of 1977, Kent State again made the headlines. Hundreds of students were protesting against the building of a gymnasium on the exact site where the killings had taken place. This time, the police remained quietly on the periphery, and no shots were fired at all.

Commenting on "Ohio" on his 1977 *Decade* album, Neil wrote: "It's still hard to believe I had to write this song. It's ironic that I capitalized on the death of these American students. Probably the biggest lesson ever learned at an American place of learning. My best C S N & Y cut. Recorded totally live in Los Angeles. David Crosby cried after this take."

Solo Star on the Rise

One of the most outstanding successes any member of C S N & Y had during 1970 was Neil's release in August of that year of his third solo album, *After the Gold Rush.* On it, he was backed by an incredible group of musicians—Crazy Horse, Greg Reeves, Steve Stills, and Nils Lofgren. The music on this album was like nothing any of them had produced so far. Neil's voice was pitched even higher than usual and he was backed on vocals by Danny Whitten, Nils, Ralph

Joseph Sia. Fillmore East, 1970

Molina and Steve. The songs are said to be inspired by the Dean Stockwell-Herb Berman screenplay titled *After the Gold Rush*. By using more than one backup group, it seems that Neil was aiming for a completely individual performance. He recorded over a period of months, with varying numbers of session musicians appearing on each song. The final result is definitely an album of rock 'n roll music, combined with the subtler flavors of folk music and the lyricism of true poetry.

After the Gold Rush created quite a splash. It was selected as a candidate for record of the year by reviewers ranging from the underground press to *Time* and *Newsweek*. It was heralded as a *tour de force* and many claimed it revealed new vistas of Neil's talents. One of the most enthusiastic of all reviewers was Robert Hilburn in the *Los Angeles Times*, September 29, 1971: "Words like lovely, beautiful and romantic cannot often be applied to rock albums, but there haven't been many rock albums like Neil Young's *After the Gold Rush*. It is a delicate, fragile jewel . . . . In the album's best moments, Young's soft, disarming voice and the crisp haunting instrumentation are almost therapeutically gentle in this time of assault rock."

After the Gold Rush earned Neil a gold record and stayed on the charts through 1971. The public loved it and seemed to agree with all the praise it received, especially with *Cue*'s James Lichtenberg, who wrote: "This album caused its own gold rush in a definitive, brilliant proof of his broad appeal . . . it is authentic Neil Young, characteristically studded with paradox and sudden shadow."

Langdon Winner, writing in *Rolling Stone*, did not care much for this album. He said *Southern Man* as a composition was "possibly one of the best things Neil Young has ever written," but he felt that the recording of it was not up to the live performances of the song. "In recent appearances with Crosby, Stills and Nash, the piece has had an overwhelmingly powerful impact on audiences. But the recording . . . fulfills very little of this promise," he observed. Most of Neil Young's fans disagreed wholeheartedly; *Southern Man* was and still is a favorite. Winner did not like Neil's voice on *After the Gold Rush* either, whereas most listeners felt Neil had taken his voice to a new height, which was amazing, considering how high-pitched he usually sang, anyway. "In his best work Young's singing contains genuine elements of pathos, darkness and mystery," wrote Winner. "If Kafka's story 'The Hunger Artist' could be made into an opera, I would want Neil Young to sing the title role . . . [but on this album] he was singing a half-octave above his highest acceptable range."

It almost didn't matter what any critic had to say, good or bad, about Neil at this point in his career. His output—and the quality of everything he was doing—had his fans in ecstasy. Songs from *After the Gold Rush*, like "Southern Man," "Till the Morning Comes," "Only Love Can Break Your

Heart," "Don't Let It Bring You Down," "Tell Me Why," and "I Believe in You," became instant favorites.

In the title song from the album "After the Gold Rush," Neil's poetic images reflect much of what was happening as the new decade began. *"Look at Mother Nature on the run / In the nineteen-seventies,"* he sings.

Striking another common chord, Neil spoke for many of us when he sang: *"But only love can break your heart / Try to be sure right from the start / . . . What if your world should fall apart."* Always concerned with love, Neil at this time was married to Susan and they seemed to have their lives very much together. But he continued to be curious about love, what it is like

Joseph Sia. With James Taylor, New York, 1970

to have it, and what it is like to be without. *"When you were young and on your own / How did it feel to be alone? / I was always thinking of games that I was playing / Trying to make the best of my time."*

"Southern Man" is accusatory and very strong in tone. The Southerner, particularly the Southern white man, was seen clearly as the villain. Hatreds and violence continued to erupt. Neil (who never actually witnessed any of it) used poetic license when he sang: *"I saw cotton and I saw black / Tall white mansions / And little shacks / Southern man when will you pay them back / I heard screaming and bullwhips cracking. . . ."*

"I Believe in You" could be dedicated to any couple who has ever gone through changes: breaking up and making up; one minute thinking you have everything figured out, the next believing that you are the crazy one; questioning, doubting, coming, and going; pulling close and pushing apart. Neil sang of the complexities in a relationship: *"Now that you've found yourself / Losing your mind are you here again / Finding that what you once thought was real is gone / And changing."* And he expressed the futile wish that it would all somehow straighten itself out when he sang: *"Coming to you at night / I see my questions, I feel my doubts / Wishing that maybe in a year or two / We could laugh and let it all out."* Neil included "I Believe in You" on *Decade*, where he summed up his feelings about the song with the cryptic statement: "I think this gets to the heart of the matter and as Danny Whitten once said, 'I don't want to talk about it.'"

It would be a year and a half before Neil released another solo album (*Harvest*, February 1972), but in between Neil could be heard on the Crosby, Stills, Nash and Young album *4 Way Street* (April, 1971). It had over $1,000,000 in sales before its release, and reached Number One on the charts in mid-May. A double album of selected songs recorded live during their concert tours in June and July of 1970, *4 Way Street* is surprisingly good. Backed by Johnny Barbata on drums and Calvin Samuels on bass, C S N & Y sang and played in the same key on practically every cut, thereby avoiding overdubbing in the studio. It is a showcase of solo material by each of the four.

"The exceptions—'Long Time Gone,' 'Pre-Road Downs,' and 'Carry On'—are still pretty ragged live, but in the latter case this is mitigated somewhat by the fact that 'Carry On' serves as the vehicle for some long, exciting Stills-Young electric exchanges," wrote George Kimball in his *Rolling Stone* review of the album. "Young and Stills also really get it on together on the other extended number (13-plus minutes), Neil's 'Southern Man,' trading off some steaming riffs which compare favorably with the Danny Whitten-Young guitar work on the original (*After the Gold Rush*) version.

"Neil Young's 'Cowgirl in the Sand' (done by himself with acoustic guitar) is a strangely different song than the recording with Crazy Horse, but it is utterly exquisite all the same. Young also does lovely acoustic solos of 'Don't Let It Bring You Down' (from *Gold Rush*) and an old Buffalo Springfield tune, 'On the Way Home.' Even 'Ohio' is no worse (though no better) than the single. . . . Crosby, Stills, Nash and Young are all performers of unquestionable talent, and—mostly because they stay out of each others' way—*4 Way Street* must surely be their best album to date."

*Crosby, Stills, Nash and Young
Split Up—For the Most Part*

4 Way Street was to be C S N & Y's last album as a group except for the release of *So Far* in 1974, which contained the best of C S N & Y. Throughout 1970 and 1971, they continued to tour together and as individuals. Any concert was always preceded by a great deal of anticipation, for the audience was never sure which of the four were going to show up. And there was always talk of another album in the works.

There was never an official announcement of the group's split, no final, one-last-time-together big bash; the four gradually went their separate ways.

In May of 1971, Neil had finished one of his tours and was working on his fourth album in Nashville. It was a painful period for him physically. He previously had slipped a disc while on tour during the year, and in Nashville he suffered another slip.

Steve Stills was getting over a nerve-racking waiting period. In August of 1970 he had been busted in La Jolla, California. The charges were originally for possession of "dangerous drugs" (cocaine and barbiturates) but were reduced later to a misdemeanor. Stills paid a $1000 fine and was put on probation. Nash and Crosby were each working on solo albums, as well as on a new duet LP.

In the fall of 1971, the four announced another tour together. That meant the audience could expect at least Crosby and Nash to show up, probably also either Stills or Young, and sometimes both Stills and Young in the same evening. When that took place, the crowd would go wild. Even though these surprise jams with all four had always been a bonus treat on their concert tours from the very beginning, the crowd just never knew what to expect. The four performers had announced that that was how it would be from the very beginning, that they never had intended to be a "group" in the accepted sense of the word. Whenever all four did get together, it was for the very basic reason that they felt like it and that it brought them a lot of joy.

Crosby and Nash usually opened the concerts and were always cheered wildly. When Stills came on stage, he most often got a standing ovation. Neil's appearance brought an even more frenzied ovation, from a crowd that was by then deleriously happy.

For these fall concerts, Stills was sometimes able to leave Miami, where he was working on a special project (his solo album, *Stephen Stills 3*) and Neil would come up from the South, where he was beginning work on his movie, *Journey Through the Past*. Three out of the four wound up one particular tour in Berkeley. When Neil walked on stage toward the end of the set, he sang "Helpless"; then he introduced "Alabama" from his soon-to-be-released album, *Harvest*. "Graham and David put down their guitars to sing gentle harmony behind Young's distinctive lonely voice," reported *Rolling Stone* on November 11, 1971. "Like most Neil Young songs, it needed hearing more than once; but some people evidently had other things in mind. Just as the last chord of 'Alabama' vibrated into silence, some pimple in the second row took advantage of the quiet to stand up and shout at the top of her voice, 'Where's Steve?' Stills was 3,000 miles away, back in Miami, and those who want to be assured of seeing C S N & Y together will have to wait until June and July when a tour is scheduled. There's a C S N & Y album in the works, too. It will probably be finished this spring, though David Crosby says he isn't holding his breath on it. It really depends on how they all *feel*, you see."

Crosby's comment proved correct, for there was no C S N & Y album that following spring or any time since. Over the next few years the four did pop up together, occasionally joining in on stage at each other's concerts, playing on each other's albums, even getting together to record for their "next" album. They have remained close as friends and have somehow always maintained their musical connection. Yet they were so torn apart by the end of 1971 that even music couldn't bring them together for any serious length of time. Still, they themselves continued to talk about a reunion. Once they even wound up together on the island of Maui in Hawaii where they worked on some new songs. It went so well that they then headed for Neil's ranch and managed to record a half-dozen songs for their "next" album. Then everything started falling apart for them again. Disagreements arose over just how to go about recording the songs; how best to present them on stage; how to work out their individual schedules and commitments in such a way as to satisfy the group's needs. The desire was there to make the commitment to the group—but somehow the egos always got in the way to prevent a permanent reunion.

However, in the summer of 1974 they did manage to regroup again, this time long enough to go on a major extended tour that received enormous amounts of attention and enthusiasm. Major cities pulled crowds of up to 200,000, with most ranging between the 40,000 to 75,000 capacity. Unofficially, the total gross estimates ranged between $6 million and $10 million. The average ticket price was $8.50 and the total number of people expected to see the shows was close to one million.

Rolling Stone's Ben Fong-Torres, obviously a fan of C S N & Y, reported on the early stages of their tour in the August 15 issue of *Rolling Stone*: "Minutes after Crosby, Stills, and Nash, and then Young, hit the stage for the first concert of their reunion tour, it was clear that no other group ever had a chance of replacing them while they were apart—not America, not Bread, not Poco, not the Eagles, not Seals and Crofts or Loggins and Messina or Souther, Hillman and Furay. Not even Manassas or the reunion of the original Byrds.

"It's been four years since the last tour, and each of the principals has gone through weighty changes. But onstage, you can hardly tell. The 1969 Woodstock language is still there; Stills and Young the fabled guitar stars. And although a couple of the voices have measurably changed, the meat of the group is still the high vocal harmonies. . . .

Jim Marshall. With Jerry Garcia & Mountain Girl, 1972

"Crosby, Stills, Nash and Young are uniquely attractive, for some obvious musical reasons and, not insignificantly, for some more mysterious personal ones. The fact that the group broke up at the height of success in 1970 was puzzling enough. That Graham Nash would later attribute the split to 'stupid, infantile ego problems' made it only more interesting, and sad. Then came the annual announcements of impending reunions, followed by almost ritual withdrawals of those announcements."

More than just a little curious as to why the group couldn't get back together and *stay* together, and wondering how they had been spending their time between 1970 and 1974, Fong-Torres went along for a good part

Neal Preston/Mirage. 1974 Tour

of the tour. He interviewed each one except for Neil, whom he only managed to talk to briefly; he had to depend on what the others could tell him to piece together Neil's 4-year history. The interviews, conversations, and observations appeared in the August 29 issue of *Rolling Stone*, in a lengthy, insightful article that brought everyone up to date on the C S N & Y phenomenon.

"Year after year," Fong-Torres wrote, "this all-time favorite group from out of the Woodstock era, these symbols of harmony in music, would try to get back and would fail. 'We really did try, every year,' Nash would say. 'It just didn't happen because it wasn't real.'"

Nash attributed their inability to regroup not only to ego problems, but more specifically to the fact that the initial split "was between me and Stephen and it was over a lady. That's why we broke up that first time."

Crosby agreed more with Nash's earlier evaluation. "Ego being out of balance with intelligent cooperation makes you impossible to work with, and some of us were more guilty than others and it's nodbody's business which ones they are." When asked about the persistent stories concerning the constant fighting between Stills and Young, Crosby replied: "It's not that simple. We're all four guilty as shit.... I could come back and forth with reasons all day, but it would sound like two high school kids arguing in homeroom about who did what to who first.... The basic thing is we all had to get to a point where we wanted to play with each other, where we felt like 'Outtasite, I want to be in a band now, I want to play and sing harmony with those guys.'" And that just did not happen, because Steve and Neil did not want to be with each other or with the other two when they did their own tours. "They were each looking for 'self-expression,'" explained Crosby.

According to Stills, the split had a lot to do with musicianship and egos. "I think we all went through a stage of growing as musicians. We went through one stage together and another separately and now we're going through another together." Steve felt he had grown up a great deal and that many of their earlier problems as a group had to do with youth. "I mean, hey, what did we all do, what the fuck were we all doing? David with The Byrds, and me and Neil with the Springfield, we were all trying to... I mean, Neil's got that beautiful song, 'Don't Be Denied.' It says '*Pretty soon, matter of fact, played guitar. Used to sit on the back porch and think about being stars....*' And that's about as far as it goes."

He even confessed to Fong-Torres just how much he missed the group when they weren't together. "I missed 'em, you know. I missed Graham telling me when to stop and what was too much and I missed David's vocals and I missed Neil's collaboration on the sound of the records. I missed playing guitar with him, 'cause we really back each other up.... I just love it, to sit there and listen to Neil tell the story, and a couple of times I had his phrase and just repeated it back to him. That kind of shit."

He and Neil were particularly close at this time. In March 1973, while Steve was living in London, he had married a popular French singer named Veronique Sanson. They had a son, Christopher. Neil was also a parent by this time. He and Susan Young had split in 1971, and Neil had begun living with actress Carrie Snodgress. They had a son whom they named Zeke, and Neil had his 1½-year-old lively baby boy with him on the tour. For Stills, the fact that they both had babies put them "in a place where we can really relate to each other. Some of the kid stuff we used to pull goes away. Just taking things the wrong way, not using your head about relationships with people."

Neil was the lone holdout when it came to talking to Fong-Torres about himself. He was always referred to as the "reluctant star" of the group, and this time proved to be no exception. He avoided all contact with the press by staying busy before each show, sticking close to the others in the group as they talked, joked, laughed, jammed, and warmed up. After each concert was finished, he would pack up his son Zeke and their dog, Art, and immediately drive away in a GMC camper van toward the next town. Manager-friend-confidant Elliot Robert has said about Neil and his reluctance to be interviewed: "Well, he just doesn't want to talk; he says he's got nothing to say.... He never likes the way he comes out in print. He says it sounds like someone else."

Neil was determined on this trip to spend as much time as possible with Zeke. This meant staying clear of airports, hotels, and anyone not directly involved with the shows. He also really liked being on the road. As Crosby told Fong-Torres, "He loves driving down the old highway." Nash added another explanation for Neil's Garbo-like reclusiveness: "He doesn't trust a lot of people."

It was in Nashville, while Neil was in town for the Johnny Cash show and to record *Harvest*, that he met bassist Tim Drummond. At 34, Drummond had already played with Conway Twitty and James Brown, becoming "the only paleface in his band." Tired of traveling, he had pretty much settled down in Nashville where he did session work; then he heard Neil needed a bassist. "So I showed up and the first song we cut was 'Heart Gold,'" he told Fong-Torres. "Later we went out to Neil's ranch (in La Honda, California, south of San Francisco) and recorded in this old barn, with bird shit all over and holes in the ceiling and a remote truck parked outside. 'Alabama' and 'Are You Ready' are from the barn."

Neil asked Drummond to join him on his next tour. He agreed, even though it meant once more hitting the road. It was through Drummond that the new band Neil was playing with got its name. When he was with

James Brown, he told Fong-Torres, "We'd be riding in a bus with James and get drunk and we'd call it 'seeing gators.' One guy would call out, 'There goes a flock of 'em, strayin' behind.'" Thus, the name Stray Gators was born.

This tour was extremely hard on Neil. They started it January 5, 1973, and in only three months' time, he and the Stray Gators had played in 65 cities. They concentrated on the big halls in each town, playing to audiences of between 15,000 and 20,000. "He looked disheveled throughout; he was criticized for doing too short a show (the average was an hour and a quarter) and he had just completed a film, *Journey Through the Past*, that would fail to secure a distribution deal and would account for his least successful album ever," wrote Fong-Torres.

"There was so much pressure on him," Drummond told the reporter. "It was just him in front of the mike." (This was true except for the last four cities, where both Crosby and Nash joined him in concert, thereby starting another rumor that they were all getting back together.)

In between this exhausting tour and the group's reunion in 1974, Neil began recording an album he called *Tonight's the Night*, then dumped the project. He was later to resurrect it, put additional work into it, and release it in 1975. But the first time around *Tonight's the Night* just didn't work. "It was a flash," says Drummond. "He wanted to use Crazy Horse, he did, and he had an album. It was done live in his studio and it sounded like an old funky club, three in the morning." Elliot Roberts added, "It was a drumken rock & roll party album." And Crosby put it simply: "He wasn't satisfied with it."

So, in the period between 1970 and the spring of 1974, Neil had come out with *Harvest, Journey Through the Past, Time Fades Away*, and had just finished recording *On the Beach* to be released in July 1974. Despite all this recording, he still had a few songs left over!

"He agreed to the reunion," wrote Fong-Torres, "and offered his ranch, nestled in the redwoods, as rehearsal quarters, six days a week throughout the month of June."

"Neil played host in the most incredible fashion," Crosby told Fong-Torres. "He built this full-size, 40-foot stage in a grove of redwoods and right across from his studios so we could record. He put half of us up and fed us all, had two chicks working. And the place, because it's so private and beautiful, was a natural to make us feel great and work hard."

Graham Nash continued: "Neil, because of his achievement on a personal level and because he's feeling comfortable with himself, is able to extend that hospitality to others. Before, he wasn't as open to doing that. He has gotten, from my own viewpoint, to gain a great deal of patience and consideration for other people."

Frederic Underhill. Courtesy Warner Bros Records; filming Journey Through the Past

Drummond added his own observations: "Neil's a changed man. He's really one of the boys now, a funky-ass musician. He's more open than he used to be. He's really into music—playing music—rather than being out front. I don't think he feels the pressure any more. Just play, and forget all that other shit."

When Fong-Torres asked Neil if he could find a half-hour or so after the show in St. Paul, Minnesota, to sit down and talk, all Neil would say was: "Well, I'm taking off right after the show, and it's a 22-hour drive to Denver. You know, I'm not real good at giving interviews. But I'll tell you, I'm having a lot of fun and it's getting better every day." And that was that.

The others were more open with Fong-Torres, as they had always been with the press. Crosby revealed: "There's a lot less hollowness, a lot less loneliness. I've had an old lady for two, three years and wider circle of friends that includes a lot of people who have nothing to do with music— boat people. And it helps balance. Music itself is wonderful but the business needs a little balance. . . . When I was with the Byrds and living in L.A., I thought that was everything that was happening in the world. But there's stuff happening out there that has nothing to do with music, concerts, money and showbiz."

Since all the others were going off on their own during these years, Crosby decided to look for his own audience. "Elliot Roberts insisted I do it," he told Fong-Torres. "He said it'd change how I felt about myself. It did. It gave me much more confidence."

"First, he [Crosby] coupled up with Nash for a month-long acoustic tour in the fall of 1971, after the first attempted C S N & Y regrouping fell through," reported Fong-Torres. "They toured again a year later, and, last fall, after another reunion dissolved, each took off for short tours through Eastern college towns, doing a half-dozen shows each."

When asked how he felt about all this touring, Crosby immediately replied, "I flat loved it, and I found all the weirdos who would come out just to see me. I found out that there is a group that likes my songs."

Unlike the other three, Graham Nash painted a rather negative portrait of himself during the period 1970-1974. Success did not bring him the same kind of satisfaction and inner harmony it seemed to have brought the others. "When C S N & Y decided that emotionally it couldn't make it as a band, that we couldn't stand each other for more than the three hours it took to play together, I retreated. First I toured with David 'cause I still had that energy. . . . But I decided that I finally really needed to find out who the fuck I was, what was important to me in terms of how much I could put up with to be able to live with myself. So I took a couple of years where I didn't do too much except finish my house (a Victorian in the Haight/Ashbury), write several songs and just stay away,'" Nash commented.

Regarding personal relationships, Nash said: "I decided I was going to try and be as honest as I could in my relationships. I changed dramatically as a person because I was always very easygoing and outward, and I'm not easygoing now.... And before, when I got depressed, I could always go to someone's room and yuk it up, just fake my way out of it. But I can't do that anymore. And girlfriends come up and hug me and I feel ... I don't know, I don't feel *any*thing. And I'm trying to figure out whether I've thought myself into a paralysis of feeling.

"There's something in me that automatically makes me do the positive thing in any given situation. It's because I've trained myself that way. The

Alvan Meyerowitz. San Francisco, 1973

bad feeling is wondering whether I really mean it or whether I'm just on automatic pilot."

Fong-Torres ventured to probe further into Nash's feelings when he brought up the concept of "self-love." Graham responded immediately, "Yeah, I've got to try and see the good things that I am. David is doing numbers on me every day, 'cause he sees me sinking and sinking." It is obvious that Graham's melancholy, depression, and boredom were getting him down. Even though all four of them had produced solo albums of definite merit, his *Wild Tales* was the only one that had failed to reach the charts. "It almost feels to me like no one heard it," he told Fong-Torres, "and that hurts for any artist trying to communicate. I haven't even asked about the sales."

Even though it was more lucrative for Crosby, Stills, and Nash, with or without Young, to stay together and make records, there seemed to be no way this would ever happen over any extended period of time. Crosby seemed to express it best for all of them when Fong-Torres asked him about the future of C S N & Y. "My guess," he said, "is that we won't stay together.... Because contrary to everybody else, who seem to want to just grind it out by the pound as fast as they humanly can—you know, 'make your hay while you can'—we like to do it when we feel like it, so that it doesn't come out sounding to you like it's been ground out by the pound. So we get together and play when it's exciting to do it—and it isn't exciting to do it all the time."

The article in *The Stars and Superstars of Rock* summed up the situation best: "Looking back, the most surprising thing about Crosby, Stills, Nash & Young was not the short space of time they stayed together, but the fact that such diverse personalities and musicians got together at all. In many ways, they were the first example of the now common phenomenon of well-known musicians getting together to play on each other's records. But unlike most of those records, at their best C S N & Y were able to spark each other off and create a fiery unity of almost frightening intensity."

Neil Young: Superstar

SHOP No 0005

Neil Young became by far the most successful member of the group. By the end of the C S N & Y tour in 1974, the sales on his solo albums had far outstripped the others' individual efforts. While *Déjà Vu* had sold 2.5 million and *4 Way Street* 900,000, Neil's solo sales were just as impressive: *Everybody Knows This Is Nowhere*, 1.3 million; *After the Gold Rush*, 1.8 million; *Harvest*, 2 million; *Journey Through the Past*, 300,000; and *Time Fades Away*, 480,000. None of the others' solo LPs hit over a million. Stills came the closest when one of his albums sold 900,000; Crosby's one solo had sales of 500,000.

Released in February 1972, *Harvest* was a smash hit, winning a gold record award during the year. One of the hit singles from the album, "Heart of Gold," was played on both middle-of-the-road and Top-40 stations. *Heart of Gold* and *Old Man* both received gold-record awards as top hit singles that year.

Harvest was Neil's strongest country record to date, with the fewest rock 'n roll influences. Besides Tim Drummond on bass, the other members of the backup band, the Stray Gators, included Ben Keith on steel guitar, Jack Nitzsche on piano and slide guitar, and Kenny Buttrey on drums. This combination of musicians created a much softer, slower sound behind Neil, whose voice was even lower, softer and smoother to match. Two songs were recorded in London ("A Man Needs a Maid" and "There's a World") and were backed by the London Symphony Orchestra to arrangements by Nitzsche. These add an overall ethereal, round, and full quality to the album, so different from Neil's previous album, *After the Gold Rush*. The rest of the songs on *Harvest* were recorded either in Nashville or in California. The first three set the tone for the entire album with their slow, country style. They are heavily autobiographical. Since he so rarely grants interviews, a lot of what happens in Neil's private life must be gleaned from his lyrics. During 1971, Neil and Susan were drifting apart, heading for a breakup. And during this same period, Neil met and fell in love with actress Carrie Snodgress, after first flipping out over her on the screen. Any period of breaking up and starting anew is difficult and painful.

For Neil, whose needs for a woman, home, stability, roots and family are so deep and overwhelming, this kind of change was particularly traumatic.

The very first song on *Harvest*, "Out on the Weekend," reflects the confusion, loneliness, and near-panic he felt as he prepared to make the final break with Susan and head out on his own—a single man once again. *"Think I'll pack it in / And buy a pick-up, Take it down to LA,"* he sings. *"Find a place to call my own / And try to fix up / Start a brand new day."* The beat is so slow, the mood so low, that the song comes out as a lament rather than a celebration. Many feel euphoric at starting a brand new day. When Neil sang "Start a brand new day," the steady, dirgelike rhythm he used suggested weariness instead. *"See the lonely boy / Out on the week-end, / Trying to make it pay / Can't relate to joy / He tries to speak and / Can't begin to say."*

A plea for sympathy? A bit of self-pity he is indulging in? An unusually intimate portrait of himself he is revealing to us? These lines reflect all of that and more. Neil was definitely the lonely boy out on the weekend looking for someone to love. And he was all the lonely people who, out of need, run to arms that open up to them, even if those arms are not the ones they ultimately want to be in. *"The woman I'm thinkin' of / She loved me all up / But I'm so down today . . . Now I'm running down the road / Trying to stay up / Somewhere in her head."*

The title song, *Harvest*, is even more country-sounding and continues with the steady, weary beat of the previous song. It is a complex song, dreamlike and perplexed, and it seems to ask the ultimate question of what to do when love has become unbalanced: *"Will I see you give more than I can take / Will I only harvest some / As the days fly past will we lose our grasp / Or fuse it in the sun?"* This is Neil's favorite record from Nashville.

John Mendelsohn reviewed *Harvest* in *Rolling Stone* on March 30, 1972. For the most part he couldn't find much to praise about it. Most people were more than delighted with Neil's laid-back, country, troubadourlike role on this album; Mendelsohn sorely missed Neil's electric guitar playing. "He's all but abdicated his position as an authoritative rock-and-roller . . . seldom playing electric guitar at all any more, and then with none of the spellbinding economy and spine-tingling emotiveness that characterized his playing with Crazy Horse," Mendelsohn observed.

He did like the third cut, however. "Only 'A Man Needs a Maid' . . . is particularly interesting," he said. This song caused quite a stir. On first hearing the lyrics, it is easy to accuse Neil of being a male chauvinist. Mendelsohn pointed this out when he wrote, "Neil treats his favorite theme—his inability to find and keep a lover—in a novel and arrestingly brazen (in terms of our society's accelerating consciousness of women's rights) manner. . . ." But, this symphony-orchestrated song is just not quite that simple on further listening. It starts off very slowly, with only a piano accompaniment, and continues with Neil's lament from the first two songs: *"My life is changing in so many ways/I don't know who to trust anymore/ There's a shadow running through my days/Like a beggar going from door to door."*

What would an easy solution to this confusion be? Just find someone to take care of you. Neil is certainly not the first or last man—or woman— who has wanted to turn to someone to be taken care of, particularly in that

transitional period when love has totally failed and he or she is all alone. With full orchestration, bells tolling, violins soaring, and horns building in crescendo, the music emphasizes and underlines the lyrics, *"It's hard to make that change/When life and love turn strange . . . and cold."*

Then we learn that another love is on the horizon. It becomes obvious that Neil wrote this song soon after falling in love at a distance with the star of a movie he went to see with friend: *"A while ago somewhere I don't know when/I was watching a movie with a friend/I fell in love with the actress/She* was playing a part that I could understand—/A maid. A man needs a maid/ When will I see you again?"

The actress was Carrie Snodgress. And the movie was *Diary of a Mad Housewife,* in which she did a magnificent job of playing the role of the totally dominated woman.

With her enormous eyes, honey-blonde hair and vibrant, husky voice, she totally captured Neil Young's heart, as well as everyone else's. "Carrie Snodgress, a nobody from Park Ridge, Illinois, captivated the critics with her unspoiled charm and luminous looks in Frank and Eleanor Perry's *Diary of a Mad Housewife,*" wrote one critic in the *New York Times* (August 19, 1977). She became an overnight star and an Oscar nominee with this, her first movie, and her future in Hollywood looked incredibly good. Then she met Neil Young and made some very important life decisions. As we listen to Neil's songs, his need for a woman to be constantly by his side, to share his life of seclusion and strenuous traveling becomes very obvious. The choice of which star to follow—her own, promising career or her new-found love, a superstar of rock—must have weighed very heavily on Carrie. In August 1977, she told a reporter that at the time (1971) she "just couldn't manage a career, raise a kid, and take care of Neil all at the same time." Neil obviously needed a great deal of taking care of . . . and he was lucky enough to get more than a maid to do the job.

In his note to "A Man Needs a Maid" on *Decade,* Neil tells us: "Some people thought this arrangement was overdone, but Bob Dylan told me it was one of his favorites. I listened closer to Bob. Robin Hood loved a maid long before women's liberation."

On "Heart of Gold," Neil and the Stray Gators get an additional boost with James Taylor and Linda Ronstadt coming in on the vocals. The tempo picks up a good bit and the harmonica, pedal steel, and good acoustic guitar work make it a strong song.

"Are You Ready for the Country?" has a grand, honky-tonk sound, made even better with additional vocals by buddies Graham Nash and David Crosby. In a way it is an "in" kind of song; one superstar singing to his other superstar friends, telling them that what they're doing is not only okay, but actually blessed: *"I was talkin' to the preacher/Said God was on my side."* But we're all going to die anyway, superstars and the rest of us, so go ahead and do what you do so well, he seems to be telling them: *"Then I ran into the hangman/He said it's time to die/You gotta tell your story boy/You know the reason why."*

James Taylor and Linda Ronstadt join in again on "Old Man," the first cut on Side Two. They come in strong on the chorus, which is really a knockout. *"Old man take a look at my life/I'm a lot like you/I need someone to love me/The whole day through/Oh, one look in my eyes/And you can tell that's true.''* Here we have it again, that deep-seated need for someone to love him.

"Old Man" was written in Neil's transition period between Susan and Carrie. Neil was going home to be consoled for losing his loved one—and to find reassurance, perhaps, that it wouldn't happen again. He was only 24 at the time; having accomplished so much in such a short period, he must have felt much older than he actually was. And at 24 he knew he still had a lot more to do. *"Twenty-four and there's so much more/Live alone in a paradise/That makes me think of two/Love lost, such a cost/Give me things that don't get lost/Like a coin that won't get tossed/Rolling home to you."*

In "There's a World," Nitzsche's extraordinary talents as an arranger come into play, backing Neil with the London Symphony Orchestra. It opens like the soundtrack to *Ben Hur*, then softens as strings start low and build back up. Flute, harp, violins weave in and around the piano and Neil's mellow voice, fading and building, fading and building like the ebb and flow of the tide. It is a beautiful song, the lyrics secondary to the music.

"Alabama" became a favorite of many, but it never reached the classic popularity of "Southern Man." The themes of both are similar—an indictment against the South. But where "Southern Man" had vivid images and strong accusations, "Alabama" is much softer in tone, more questioning. And its lyrics do not have the poetic imagery of the first song. It lacks the driving force, the strength of conviction, the emotionalism of "Southern Man." Perhaps more understanding, a softening of the anger had taken place: *"Alabama—you got the weight on your shoulders/That's breaking your back,"* he sings in the first stanza, and winds up offering a bit of optimism and hope in the last lines, *"You got the rest of the union to help you along/What's going wrong?"*

As most rock stars would agree, the problem of drugs in their world is a major one. Neil never got into any heavy drugs, but he did witness the destruction of many who did.

"The Needle and the Damage Done" is a minor song, very short, recorded live at UCLA. It is just Neil singing and playing acoustic guitar, and the only poetic line is the last: *". . . every junky's like a setting sun."* But it must have meant something more to Neil, for it is a very personal song. He seems to have just lost a much-loved friend to a drug overdose: *"I watched the needle take another man/Gone, gone. The damage done./I sing the song because I love the man/I know that some of you don't understand/Milk-blood to keep from running out."* A few years later he came out with a much stronger indictment against drugs on "Tonight's the Night" (July 1975).

Steve Stills joined Graham Nash on additional vocals for the last cut of the album, "Words/(Between the Lines of Age)." It is one of the most difficult to understand of Neil's songs, the meaning obscured in oblique phrases and images. It is the longest song on the album (6:42 minutes), and he does play an extended electric guitar solo on it. It is uneven and even his solo work seems hesitant and clumsy.

The best thing that reviewer Mendelsohn had to say about *Harvest* had to do with Neil's voice. After listening to the album for a dozen times, he came up with "only one happy thing to say about it: Neil Young still sings awful pretty, and often even touchingly." Two million people liked it a lot more than Mendelsohn, and for a lot more reasons than just the fact that Neil sang awfully pretty on it. As one writer in *The Rolling Stone History of Rock and Roll* said about Neil's *After the Gold Rush* and *Harvest*: "With [these two albums], Young seemed to be attaining some modicum of self-knowledge and self-mockery; 'A Man Needs a Maid' was an interesting morass of conflicting impulses. And the musical primitivism into which he had by then settled carried a nicely complimentary irony; as Young's ideas about himself grew more tangled, he fought back by offsetting them with clean, lucid instrumentation."

A Journey Through the Past on Film

From the high generated by *Harvest*, Neil took a dive to his lowest point with *Journey Through the Past*, released in November 1972. The album was recorded as a soundtrack to the film of the same name; neither was a success for Neil, but at least the film was more interesting. It premiered at the US Film Festival in Dallas, Texas, April 8, 1973. One of the few critics to cover the film was Bob Porter, who wrote for the *Dallas Times-Herald*:

"*Journey Through the Past* comes off as sort of a cinematic contemplation of the navel. The film will probably disappoint those fans seeking the music of Young and be of value primarily to those searching souls looking for a view of the outside world from inside the hectic, confused, and confusing world of rock music."

That was very accurate. The music was a disappointment, but the "inside" look at the world of rock music did prove to be interesting. However, as a film, it brought gentle criticism from Porter: "It seems at odds that someone so organized and craftsmanlike in his music would approach another media so unstructured. Young expressed the determination to do other films. He is artist enough that he may grow with that. With *Journey* he stands as a filmmaker somewhat like he would as a beginning musician."

The 1973 US Film Festival did not pull a very large crowd, but the showing of Neil's film drew the largest audience of the week. The few celebrities on hand that week showed up, including Vincent Minnelli, Jack Nicholson, Lou Adler, and Neil's very own Carrie Snodgress (who, true to their life-style, had with her their son Zeke, six months old at the time).

Neil explained the film and the title to Janelle Ellis, who reported on it

Frederic Underhill. Courtesy of Warner Bros Records

for *Rolling Stone* (May 24, 1973): "Basically, the film is about me. It's a collection of thoughts. Every scene meant something to me—although with some of them I can't say what."

Producer Fred Underhill, who had also worked on documentaries *Marjoe* and *Woodstock*, tried to expand: "He ventured into fantasy, and did fictional sequences. But it also had his music and some historical context for it, from TV films of Buffalo Springfield through today."

Janelle Ellis did the best job anyone could do in summing up the "plot" of the movie. She described it for *Rolling Stone* in the following manner:

"Young's thoughts are expressed through a character known as the Graduate, played by Richard Lee Patterson, who appears throughout the film. In one Fellini-like sequence, the man, in cap and gown, gets beaten senseless, he's dropped off in the middle of a desert, and from there begins to wander; the church, the military and big business are portrayed as the main threats to his constitutional rights. Later, there is a morbidly drawn-out scene of a junkie fixing up (Neil later indicated that he had witnessed such scenes backstage); shots of Jesus Freaks on Hollywood Boulevard putting the word on Young; and a recreation of a recurring dream of his: twelve black-hooded men on black horses sweeping down a beach toward a man and his pickup truck. Although Young said he couldn't explain its significance, the scene serves as the illustration for the soundtrack album.

"Another scene has Young in a junkyard under a busy freeway. He sits in a '57 Buick, opens his lunchbox and talks ecology: 'Like, man, you know, rebuilding old cars instead of manufacturing new ones.' . . . He also sent to TV networks in New York to look through stock footage; coming up with, among others, ABC-TV's coverage of Billy Graham and Richard Nixon at a youth rally in the South, singing 'God Bless America' together."

Neil did most of the work on the movie. He is credited as editor, he directed scenes and conceived of most of the film's fantasy bits. The movie is identified as "A film by Neil Young."

When his name flashed on the screen at the showing in Dallas, the audience burst into applause. When the film ended, the applause was less spirited, but Neil, who had been watching from the projectionist's booth, unbeknownst to the crowd, felt the response was warm enough to come forward. He had insisted all week that there be no press coverage about his being at the festival, so when he bounded down the aisle toward the stage, the audience was not only surprised but delighted.

"He sat on the edge of the stage, legs dangling over the front row," Ellis reported. "'Not used to this,' Neil began. 'We don't have question-and-answer periods after our concerts.'"

The audience fell in love with him immediately and for a half-hour questioned him on everything from what he was drinking in the jug in the movie to how much the film cost (according to Underhill, about $350,000), to what was the news on C S N & Y (he tactfully ignored all questions about music—he was there to talk about his film).

"Young appeared hyper-excited through the session," Ellis wrote, "like a high-school kid who'd just won in the Science Fair, but still nervous over his first film."

Most of Neil's friends felt the film was a "decent first try." "It was a nice film," Lou Adler told Ellis. "Neil's touch is great, as it is in his music." Faithful Elliot Roberts was also on hand for the premiere and said, "This film is not as proficient as his next endeavor. But it was made with a lot of care and love."

The soundtrack was not received nearly as warmly as the film was; many felt it was taking advantage of fans who would unknowingly rush out to buy any Neil Young album, and who would presume from the title,

Journey Through the Past, that it was a retrospective of the various phases of his career. It is a retrospective in a sense but nothing with Crazy Horse is included on the album, and the best work is the earliest stuff by The Buffalo Springfield.

Journey Through the Past is a 2-record set that lasts just a little over an hour. It opens with a very funny introduction to The Buffalo Springfield, recorded during an appearance they had made on a television show. There is a lot of applause and the group sings "For What It's Worth," then moves immediately into "Mr. Soul," recorded from the same television show. (Writing in *Rolling Stone*, March 1, 1973, Jim Miller had the kindest words to say about *Journey Through the Past* when he wrote about "Mr. Soul:" "Neil's driving vocal and guitar work on 'Mr. Soul' possess a vitality almost completely absent from *Journey*'s other cuts.")

The album continues with another great round of applause after "Mr. Soul" and then comes the recording of "Rock 'n Roll Woman," also by the Springfield. After this there are sounds of the audience, noisy and talkative, and of the group telling them to be quiet.

The first side winds up with a concert version of Crosby, Stills, Nash and Young doing "Find the Cost of Freedom" and "Ohio" (both available on *4 Way Street* in similar live versions). Side Two of *Journey* contains a concert version of "Southern Man" and a new take of "Alabama," plus some takes from the Stray Gators. Side Three is made up solely of a 15-minute-long version of "Words."

There is only one new song on *Journey*, and it is on Side Four—a solo by Neil on piano, called "Soldier." The rest of Side Four includes sounds of a man in the street talking about the kingdom of heaven. There are traffic noises in the background and repeated mention of something about relativity invitation. Handel's *Messiah* and the theme from *King of Kings*, plus Brian Wilson's instrumental "Let's Go Away for Awhile" from one of the Beach Boys' albums, make up the rest of Side Four.

All in all, a rather puzzling album, which undoubtedly deserved the low sales and even lower comments it received. Jim Miller was particularly disappointed, because he had praised Neil and hated to see him hit such a low. He commented: "Neil Young has been involved in a lot of memorable rock music over the last seven years. He was one of the most interesting songwriters in Buffalo Springfield, and his own solo work with Crazy Horse still sounds fresh today. At his best, Young transformed his thin voice into a distinctive vehicle for a haunting, frail style, while his lead guitar bristled with a concise energy. His most satisfying work . . . captured an intimate presence that was both unassuming and engaging."

SHOP № 0006
"The Man Takes Big Chances"

Neil had a busy spring in 1973; the month before the premiere of his film in Dallas, he had appeared in a solo concert with the Stray Gators at Carnegie Hall in New York. His performances always evoked mixed feelings from his audience and from reviewers and music critics. His voice could occasionally be shrill, flat and grating in some acoustic guitar solos. Then he would sing beautifully, dazzling audiences with new songs and thrilling them with their old favorites. Jon Landau reported on this concert for *Rolling Stone* of March 1, 1973. He had some mixed reactions to Neil in performance, but still came away from the concert admiring him for the person he was, as well as for the performer. Neil's independence, his tough-mindedness, his fairness, and his sensitive insights into himself and the world of rock superstardom are especially evident in one of the autobiographical songs he performed that evening, "Don't Be Denied," to be released soon thereafter on *Time Fades Away*. In this song, wrote Jon Landau, Neil "offers one of the few attacks on the star system that a rock musician has made creditable. And he makes it so because his performance and style seem free of any taint of cynicism. He knows everything the pop world has to offer and intends to enjoy himself in spite of it. As for the people who at one time or another think they are using him—whether in his professional or personal life—he doesn't even seem to mind, because he knows that while he isn't going to change them, they haven't changed him either."

When Neil sings to his audiences the songs they know and love the most, he usually is at his best. For Landau, his performance that evening proved to be no exception to this general rule. "Young hit his peak with the most familiar songs," Landau wrote, "including an explosive rendition of 'Cinnamon Girl', an improved 'Everybody Knows This Is Nowhere' and a solid 'Southern Man.' For me, everything was overshadowed by one song—'Alabama.' I think it has the best chorus he has written and in performance it builds with a majestic sway characteristic of the Rolling Stones at their best."

Over the summer and into the fall, Neil continued to perform and to record for his new album, *Time Fades Away*, released in October 1973. He used much of the new material from this album for the grand opening of the Roxy Theater in Los Angeles on September 20. After many delays and hang-ups, this long-awaited club—competition for the Troubadour and the Whisky—finally opened with Neil Young as the headliner for two shows a night for four completely sold out nights. Everyone who could get into town was there those nights, and crowds lined up on Sunset Strip to stare and shriek and reach out for celebrities including Jackson Browne, Elton John, Carole King, Helen Reddy, Herb Alpert, Bob Dylan, and Alice Cooper.

Even dressed in his customary disarray—this evening in a white sports coat several sizes too large, loosely covering an ordinary T-shirt that wasn't tucked in—Neil's presence on stage was still incredibly powerful. Backed by Nils Lofgren on guitar and vocals, Ben Keith on pedal steel, Ralph Molina on drums, and Billy Talbot on bass, Neil performed only new songs, which is not always a favorite type of performance for audiences, who love to hear familiar tunes. And very often, it takes several listenings to fall in love with a Neil Young piece. But, hidden behind dark glasses, Neil did give the crowd of 500 a powerful rendition of "Tonight's the Night," the song he wrote about Bruce Berry, a former C S N & Y roadie who had recently died of a heroin overdose.

The horror of watching helplessly as heroin took its toll of other stars and close friends was weighing heavily on Neil during this time in his life. He expressed much of this anguish in the title song on his album *Time Fades Away*. The images are bleak. "*Fourteen junkies too weak to work / One sells diamonds for what they're worth / Down on pain street, disappointed lurks.*" The sound is honky-tonk piano and harsh harmonica. The feeling is Dylanesque, and the mood of how grotesque and hopeless the junkie situation is heightens in the chorus. It is a "sharply ironic chorus," wrote Bud Scoppa in *Rolling Stone* (January 3, 1974), "in which the junkie's weak parent whines: 'Son, don't be home too late, try to get back by eight. Son, don't wait 'til the break of day 'cause you know how time fades away. . . .' The lyric is energized by hard, jerking instrumental work from the Stray Gators and by Young's jagged, piercing vocal: He's still the best whiner in rock & roll. And he expresses anguish like no one else."

"Don't Be Denied" was one of Landau's favorites from Neil's Carnegie Hall performance; it was also Scoppa's favorite song on the *Time Fades Away* album. It's a quiet, personal song, completely autobiographical. The first part deals with Neil's childhood. "In this section," wrote Scoppa,

Michael Zagaris. 1973

"Young cuts rapidly through scenes that depict the private trials of a rather delicate kid in a rugged land. This song seems an explicit re-expression of the emotional content of Young's moving but impenetrably private 'Broken Arrow.'"

In the last part of the song, Neil deals with the problems of being a star, particularly a rock star. As Landau had written, this piece in performance had "left him screaming about the paranoia that comes from '. . . seeing the world through a businessman's eyes.'" The child who dreamed of being a star finally grew up to become one, and stardom had its garish nightmares no less than childhood did. Now the crowds gathered around him were not tough bullies ready to beat up on him because he was different. They were people crowding around who were there not only to see and hear him because he was indeed different, but also to profit from that uniqueness and to walk away from the performance taking some of him with them.

"Don't Be Denied" recalls: *"The businessmen crowd around / They came to hear the golden sound / There we were on the Sunset Strip / Playing our songs for the highest bid."* While he was young and in a band, Neil played all night for practically nothing, still dreaming of being a star. Neil the star would never have to be deprived monetarily again: *"We played all night / The price was right."* He sees the flaws and dangers in being a star quite clearly though, and even as you sense his paranoia, you know that Neil is too solid and independent and honest a man to be swept away completely: *"Well, all that glitters isn't gold / I know you've heard that story told / But I'm a pauper in a naked disguise / A millionaire through a businessman's eyes."*

The conflict between the public and private Neil Young, between the star and the sequestered man, was something he had to deal with day in and day out. "Young's privateness has always been at the heart of his writing and performing," wrote Scoppa, "right alongside his staunch moral sense. These two elements have been both his prime virtues and his main flaws." Both of these elements come into play on *Time Fades Away*; the result is an uneven but positive and "startingly unorthodox album." "*Time Fades Away* is an idiosyncrasy from one of rock's most idiosyncratic artists . . . a revealing self-portrait by an always fascinating man," Scoppa concluded.

"Journey Through the Past," "Love in Mind," and "The Bridge" are beautiful, delicate love songs with Neil singing alone to his own, simple piano accompaniment. "L.A.," on the other hand, is a sarcastic diatribe against the "city in the smog." "Yonder Stands the Sinner" is a Rolling Stones type of song; Neil tends to scream in it, and sounds very disapproving. "Last Dance" is the last song on the album. Long and contemplative, the recurring chorus sounds somehow positive: *"You can live your own life / Making it happen. / Working on your own time / Layed back and laughin'."*

Neal Preston/Mirage. 1974

Joseph Stevens. CSN & Y and Jimmy Page, 1974

Chuck Pulin. Nassau, 1973

In an interview that Neil gave to Bud Scoppa for the *New Musical Express* of June 28, 1975, he looked back on *Time Fades Away* and some of his other albums recorded after *After the Gold Rush*. Scoppa questioned Neil on how he felt about them, whether he felt they were forced or dishonest in any way. Neil was emphatic that he liked his earlier albums very much and was very happy he had made them. "*Time Fades Away* sounds nervous, but even that says where I was at, because it's a direct, ah, non-hit, a direct miss. It was like a live album of songs that no one had ever heard before done in a totally different style from that one that came before it. But it stood for where I was at during that period. I was nervous and not quite at home in those big places."

This is in direct contrast to how he had felt less than two years earlier while recording *Harvest*. "Everybody said that *Harvest* was a trip. To me, I'd happened to be in the right place at the right time to do a really mellow record that was really open, 'cause that's where my life was at the time. But that was only for a couple of months. If I'd stayed there, I don't know where I'd be right now—if I'd just stayed real mellow. I'm just not that way any more. I think *Harvest* was probably the finest record that I've made, but that's really a restricting adjective for me. It's really *fine* . . . but that's it."

On the Beach was Neil's next solo album to be released (July 1974); actually, he had already recorded and mixed everything on *Tonight's the Night* in August 1973, before he had even started *On the Beach*. He didn't release *Tonight's the Night* until July 1975, however, two years after recording it; it took that long for the album to fall into place for Neil. The order of songs was important and the album just had to wait until the order worked itself out.

"*Tonight's the Night* didn't come out right after it was recorded because it wasn't finished, it just wasn't in the right space, it wasn't in the right order, the concept wasn't right," Neil told Scoppa. "I had to get the color right, so it was not so down that it would make people restless. I had to keep jolting every once in a while to get people to wake up so they could be lulled again. It's a very fluid album. The higher you are, the better it is. And it really lives up to that, a lot of records don't . . . you should listen to it late at night."

Scoppa said he did listen to it at night and afterwards couldn't get to sleep. "It scared the hell out of me," he told Neil. Neil responded to this admission with a pleased expression. "That's great. That's the best thing you could tell me."

Neil had been greatly affected by the overdose death of Bruce Berry, for whom "Tonight's the Night" was written, and the subsequent death of close friend and leader of Crazy Horse, Danny Whitten, also of an overdose of heroin. The album spooked a lot of people; it's all in black and white, even the label on the record itself, and a black space has been filled in on the back cover of the album, where Danny's picture would have been. The dedication reads: "This album was made for Danny Whitten and Bruce Berry, who lived and died for rock and roll."

Throughout 1973, Neil was touring and recording with his new version of Crazy Horse, Nils Lofgren, Ben Keith, Billy Talbot and Ralph Molina, and the tour came to be known as the Tonight's-the-Night tour. Reports of the tour always carried the word that it was bizarre, with Neil in his bitterness and despair seemingly driven to expunge the effects that the two deaths were having on him. Just as on the album, where the song appears first and last, "Tonight's the Night" was performed in varying versions two and three times a night on stage, each time chilling audiences with the horror of it all. People were saying that Neil was destroying himself on stage. For so private a man, the act of publicly pouring out his grief may have come as a relief. The audiences' discomfort was obvious. They had come to hear their favorite Neil Young's songs. They were seeing and hearing a man who was acting very strange, a man they loved and to whom they were extremely loyal. The man who had reached superstardom with the 2-million seller *Harvest* seemed to be rejecting everything that had brought him to that peak and to be changing in front of their very eyes. It was almost as though he were starting all over again, working and reworking his music and his life to change and grow as he searched for some deeper truths within himself.

This seems to be what was actually happening to Neil. He talked to Scoppa about how he felt when he got down to recording the album after all the touring. "I think what was in my mind when I made that record was I just didn't feel I was a lonely figure with a guitar or whatever it is that people see me as sometimes. I didn't *feel* laid back—I just didn't feel that way. So, I thought I'd just forget about all that and . . . wipe it out. Be as aggressive and as abrasive as I could to leave an effect, a long term effect, that things change radically sometimes—it's good to point that out. . . .

"It's just that there was a lot of spirit flyin' around when we were doin' it. It was like a tribute to those people, you know? Only the ones we chose no one had really heard of that much, but they meant a lot to us. That's why it gets spooky, 'cause we *were* spooked. If you felt that, I'm glad, because it was there . . . . The first horror record, a horror record."

Even as late as 1977, Neil still felt strongly about this album. He included it on *Decade* along with this statement: "I think this is one of my strongest and longest lasting albums. It covers my obsession with the ups and downs of the drug culture. Coincidentally, it was my least commercially successful record ever made."

The *Tonight's the Night* album was also one of Neil's favorites because it had the tone and feel of a live performance. Even though it was done in the studio, it was recorded with everybody playing and singing at the same time, with no overdubbing on any of the songs. "That's the way the old blues people used to do it," he says. The mixes were done right away and are as unorthodox as Neil's concert performances had become. Neil explained why to Bud Scoppa: "It's real music. Sometimes I'd be on the mike and sometimes I'd be two feet off it. Sometimes I'd be lookin' around the room and singin' back off-mike . . . we'd have to bring it way back up in the mix to get it. And you can hear the echo in the room. We were all on the

Neal Preston/Mirage. CSN & Y, Los Angeles, 1974

stage at S.I.R. (L.A.'s Studio Instrument Rentals) just playing, with the P.A. system and everything, just like a live thing. And all the background vocals are live. . . ."

Many people, on first hearing *Tonight's the Night*, react the same way Neil did when he first heard it after the mixes. "That's the most out-of-tune thing I've ever heard," was his initial response. On certain numbers, the harmonica, vocals, and even the piano are out of tune. Stephen Holden began his *Village Voice* review of July 7, 1975, by pointing this out: "Neil Young's *Tonight's the Night* flouts every standard of commercial recording. Its sound verges on the monophonic. The vocals are off pitch, and so are the instrumentals, which feature former Crazy Horse members Nils Lofgren, Ralph Molina, and Billy Talbot. All 11 compositions are raw, to say the least, and their stream-of-consciousness execution is about as far away from progressive radio as possible."

Holden recognized that the album was liable to alienate all but the most dedicated Neil Young fans, as well as "insult the smug, laid-back image of Southern California rock, with its ad-slick invitations to carefree hedonism." He summed it up this way: "*Tonight's the Night* thus stands diametrically opposed to all the new state-of-the-art rock & roll albums from members of the L.A. rock pantheon—Stephen Stills, Souther-Hillman-Furay, Eagles, Roger McGuinn, and Poco. Of the six, it's the only one that's emotionally compelling."

Overdubbing would have corrected the rawness and mistakes, but Neil left everything in. And somehow it works. On second hearing, Neil became convinced that the songs worked; the people who were listening with him reinforced that conviction. They started going nuts when they heard it, telling him that this was it, why hadn't he released it, and that it was so terrific he would have to worry about what to put out after this. "So it's fascinating to me, it was all just an experiment," he concluded.

Perhaps because it was recorded the way the old blues people did their recordings, perhaps because its major theme is death, much of *Tonight's the Night* sounds like rhythm and blues and old Dixieland funeral marches. Neil explained to Bud Scoppa: "What we were doing was playing those guys [Whitten and Berry] on their way. We all got that high—not *that* high, but we got as close as we could. I mean, I'm not a junkie and I won't even try it out to check out what it's like. But we'd get really high—drink a lot of tequila, get right out on the edge, where we knew we were so screwed up that we could easily just fall on our faces, and not be able to handle it as musicians. But we were wide open also at that time—just wide open. So we'd just wait until the middle of the night until the vibe hit us and just do it. We did four or five songs on the first side all in a row one night, without any break. We did 'Tonight's the Night,' 'World on a String,' 'Mellow My Mind,' 'Speakin' Out,' and 'Tired Eyes,' without any break between 'em."

Holden had guessed this is what happened and pointed it out in his review: " . . . The album sounds as though it were recorded in single takes in a desert shack in the early hours of the morning with all participants stoned to the gills. The reckless spontaneity of this approach conforms perfectly with Young's material—tales of drug-related violence and death and dope fantasy spewed out in impotent rage and hopeless confusion. While the lyrics for two love songs, 'Speakin' Out' and 'New Mama', offer a certain degree of levity, their delivery is also uncomfortably tense and in keeping with the spirit of the whole."

The delivery and sequence of the songs had a lot to do with the overall spirit of the album. The order in which it was recorded was changed many times by Neil and by Elliot Roberts. One reason Roberts was so concerned with the sequence is that he had in mind at the time a Broadway show for *Tonight's the Night*. He had a script written, put the songs in different se-

quences, and picked out other songs to be included on the album. The show never got off the ground, but the album took shape over a period of years, during which the sequence of songs was shuffled and reshuffled until they finally fell into the right place. "I made all kinds of lists to get them in the right order," Neil told Scoppa, "so that all the songs would set the other ones up, mentally, for people.

"I wanted to get the album so it could be played while people were . . . see, it's not to sit and listen to every song—eventually, people are gonna do that and that'll be cool. But the thing the album is made for is to be able to put it on once you know the songs—or even if you don't know the songs— and have the moods of it, that it takes you through subliminally, enable you to stop talking with your friends for a few minutes, start talking again and not feel uptight, enable you to flow. So that as it plays over and over it constantly changes and you don't get uptight, you know? I mean, a lot of the sequencing was made for that reason, as well as trying to get it so that if you sit there and scrutinize it, it tells a story that really makes sense."

The story *Tonight's the Night* tells in the order that it tells it is the story of death and life and death, as personally experienced by Neil himself. Elliot Roberts pointed this out to Bud Scoppa: "They're threads of life. Although Neil's portraying a character, the character he's portraying saw all those things go down."

So the album begins with death in the title song, "Tonight's the Night," the sound of which is as haunting and seductive as the message is harsh. Neil paints a portrait of someone he obviously knows well. *"Bruce Berry was a working man./He used to love that Econoline van./A sparkle was in his eye but his life was in his hand."* A working man, yes; he was a roadie for C S C S N & Y and for Crazy Horse, and took care of Steve Stills' and Neil's amps and guitars. But did he also have dreams of being a star? *"Late at night when the people were gone/he used to pick up my guitar, and sing a song/in a shaky voice that was as real as the day is long."* We won't ever get a chance to hear Bruce sing, however, *"'Cause people let me tell you,/sent a chill up and down my spine,/when I picked up the telephone and heard that he'd died out on the mainline."* That last line comes as a shocker, even though the song builds to this inevitable climax.

Neil moves us right back into life in the next song, *Speakin' Out*, with its Fats Domino-style piano, and fifties solid, steady beat. If Neil ever made dedications, this one would be for Carrie. *"I've been a searcher. I've been a fool./I've been a long time comin' to you,/hopin' for your love to carry me through./You're holding my baby, and I'm holding you./And, it's all right."*

The rest of the album continues with the ebb and flow of life and death, highs and lows, changes and doubts and affirmations, pulling us in, pushing us back, creating just the effects Neil had intended. In "World on a String," he confesses to a certain amount of ennui: *"It's just a game you see me play./Only real in the way that I feel from day to day."*

"Borrowed Tune" is a slow song with a very nice harmonica introduction and Neil on piano accompanying his own solo vocals. It's a self-deprecating song, written while on tour for *Time Fades Away*. *"I'm climbing this ladder, my head in the cloud./I hope that it matters. I'm having my doubts,"* he sings in the chorus. With the voluminous output of songs to Neil's credit, you wonder why he winds this one up with: *"I'm singin' this borrowed tune I took from the Rolling Stones./Alone in this empty room, too wasted to write my own."* Part of the enigma of the man are his parodies in his lyrics. He sings of getting so spaced out and wasted that he can't write; the reality is that he'll probably never get to recording all the songs he's already written.

The next song adds to the album's spookiness. "Come on Baby Let's Go Downtown" features Danny Whitten on vocals. It was recorded much earlier than any of the other songs—at a 1970 concert at the Fillmore East with Neil backed by Crazy Horse. Neil chose to include it on the album and in this sequence because it was so high and fast. It is indeed the fastest on the album, requiring several listenings to catch what Danny is singing. Then the message becomes clear: "*Sure enough they'll be sellin' stuff/when the moon begins to rise./Pretty bad when you're dealing with the man,/and the light shines in your eyes.*"

About the next song, Neil told Scoppa, in seeming seriousness: "If you get a hundred yards away from 'Mellow My Mind,' it sounds incredible—better than anything else sounds at a hundred yards. It's supposed to be part of the environment. Play it loud, but stay in the other room." This is one of the more out-of-tune songs with harmonica lead-in and Neil's voice taking on different fluctuations. When he first sings "*Baby, mellow my mind,/make me feel like a schoolboy on good time,*" he sings it straight. The last time around he actually sounds like a very young child, pleading in a babylike voice.

In "Roll Another Number," a country-and-western song that opens Side Two, Neil's voice drops to an all-time low which is fascinating to hear because he sounds so different when he sings that way. This is especially true in the last verse, when he sings, or rather talks, to us in that peculiarly C & W conversational style: "*I'm goin' back to Woodstock for a while,/though I long to hear that lonesome hippie smile./I'm a million miles away from that helicopter day./Oh, I don't believe I'll be goin' back that way.*" In the first verse, you can tell by the slur that he's as high as a kite, drunk as can be. It's perfect, the way he sounds; as though he is acting out the verse he is singing: "*It's too dark to put the keys in my ignition,/and the morning sun has yet to climb my hood ornament./But, before too long, my mind sees those flashing red lights./Look out, mama, 'cause I'm coming home tonight.*"

In the plaintive "Albuquerque," Neil maintains his low singing voice, sounding every bit like any other vocalist singing within a normal range of notes. This song is a flight fantasy with an ironic twist, the tale of a man fed up with what has been going down in his life and in much need of escape, who in order to get going has got to "roll another number." "*I got time to roll a number and rent a car,*" he sings, carrying the image from the chorus of the previous song. "*I been flyin' down the road/and I been starvin' to be alone,/independent from the scene that I've known.*" That need is universal; most listeners can relate to times when they have just had to get away from the turmoil and confusion in their lives. But a public figure will relate to the last line: "*I'll find somewhere where they don't care who I am.*"

Then it's back to stability and things being just fine with "New Mama," obviously a song for Carrie Snodgress. "*New mama's got a son in her eye,*" he sings. "*No clouds are in my changing sky. / Each morning when I wake up to rise, / I'm living in a dreamland.*" It's a beautiful song, very positive in its poetic images: "*Changing times, / Ancient reasons that turn to lies. / Throw them all away. / Head in hand. / Gift of wonders to understand / and open all the way.*"

"As it approaches its close," wrote Stephen Holden, "Tonight's the Night becomes progressively more ominous, injecting two scarifying explorations of dope, paranoia, betrayal, and rip-off, 'Lookout Joe' and 'Tired Eyes,' before reprising the title song."

"Lookout Joe" reaches out and startles us with its hard-rock, driving lead guitar and pounding piano—the perfect contrast to the balladlike "New Mama." "Lookout Joe" has special meaning for Neil. It was written and recorded at his ranch while they were rehearsing to go on tour for the *Time Fades Away* album. This was just after Whitten had O.D.'d. "He'd been working on the song with us and after he died we stopped for a while. When we started playing again, that was the first thing we cut and I wrote 'Don't Be Denied' that day. So 'Lookout Joe' is one of the oldest songs on the album," Neil told Bud Scoppa.

It is also the sleaziest story. Images of whores and pimps and rip-off artists and drug addicts bombard the senses and drag you into the world where low-life reigns supreme. "*A hip drag queen and a sidewalkin' street wheeler comin' down the avenue,*" he begins. "*Now, all your friends become your lovers. / There's a load of them waitin' for you.*" And he hits the nadir at the end: "*Remember Bill from up on the hill? / A cadillac put a hole in his arm. / Good old Bill, he's up there still, / havin' a ball rollin' to the bottom.*"

Never letting up, Neil drives his point home even harder in "Tired Eyes." Since the whole album is made up of Neil's own intensely personal experiences, Bud Scoppa was curious about the scene re-created in this song. It is a "straightforward description of a dope-dealing vendetta that ends in bloodshed," Scoppa wrote, then wondered if Neil had actually witnessed that sort of thing.

"Yeah," Neil responded, "puts the vibe right there . . . that's what I was sayin', at S.I.R. we were playing, and these two cats . . . who had been a *close* part of our unit—our force and our energy—were both gone to junk—both of them O.D.'d."

If the scene in "Lookout Joe" is sleazy, the scene in "Tired Eyes" is grisly. It opens with a man gunned down in a cocaine deal, then left lying in an "*open field full of old cars with bullet holes in the mirrors.*" A junkie in a junk yard. "*Well, it wasn't supposed to go down that way,*" the song goes on. "*But they burned his brother, you know, / and they left him lyin' in the driveway / and they let him down with nothing.*" / "*Well, tell me more, tell me more,*" someone insists. "*I mean, was he a heavy doper / or was he just a loser? / He was*

a friend of yours. / What do you mean, he had bullet holes in his mirrors?" The refrain, the response to these shattering experiences is the same throughout the song: *"He tried to do his best, but he could not."* This seems to be the only explanation Neil can find for such a grotesque and agonizing death.

Bud Scoppa explored "Tired Eyes" and just how and why it is successful, even in its grimness. "Young's continuing mastery of melody and texture serves his story well, although not at all in an obvious way. His musical strengths, even presented as rough sketches, provide one reason for hanging on through this grim tale in the first place. As grisly as 'Tired Eyes' seems, as abrasively as it's sung, the melody is there. Done with refinement, this would be a pretty song. Young must go to extremes to keep from making pretty music."

Neil agrees with Scoppa, and goes on to explain: "There's always a chance that nobody will dig it because it's too abrasive. But it's a very happy record if you're loose. If you're not loose, it's not happy 'cause you realize how tight you are when you listen to it. You really feel how different you are from being loose. It makes you feel something, it draws a line somewhere. I've seen it draw a line everywhere I've played it. Some people fall to one side, others fall to the other side. It's a surprise. People who thought that they'd never dislike anything I ever did, fall on the new side of the line. Other people who couldn't hear me, who said 'that cat is too sad—he sings funny'—those people listen another way now."

Neil closes the album with "Tonight's the Night," as though he were making one last attempt to purge and atone for the death of his friends. The album as a whole explores and reveals the darkest side of Neil and his obsessive fatalism. It was never a big commercial success and did, in fact, turn many away from him musically. But the album works overall for Holden, and he explains why in his review: "On one level, *Tonight's the Night* is an anti-heroin album in which Young's protagonist graphically acts the part of a strung-out, nearly incoherent drug casualty. More generally, it acknowledges the darkest consequences of the do-your-own-thing etchic. Most devastatingly, it rejects all of the satisfactions of Young's own past: his stardom, his 'Sugar Mountain' nostalgia for adolescence, and the togetherness myth of the counterculture which he helped to perpetuate. . . . Like the abstract expressionist painters and poets of whom Young has always seemed to me to be a spiritual heir, *Tonight's the Night* leaves behind a totally non-cosmetic record—in this case, a canvas of agonized grief and remorse. For Young to release the album seems almost an act of cruelty to his audience, and self-destructive as well. Whatever the reason, *Tonight's the Night* also stands as a great and troubling pop music wake."

Although it was such a downer for everyone else, Neil liked the album so much that he actually promoted it, submitting to press interviews and radio talk shows. One reason is that he had lived with it so long; other albums were recorded and released very quickly—this one took shape over two years' time. The other reason is that for the first time, Neil got to tell a complete story and to act out the parts. Bud Scoppa picked up on this aspect of the album when interviewing Neil. "*Tonight's the Night* contains all the dark, tense melancholy we've come to expect from Young's music," he wrote, "but there's one important difference. Whereas most of his serious songs have evoked their shadowy moods through indirection—recurring metaphors of flying and dancing, for example, and the mysterious Indian of 'Broken Arrow'—these songs work through explicit narrative details. Young has become a story teller, an actor."

Neil was delighted Scoppa had been sensitive to this fact, and warmed up to a lengthy discussion of what the experience was like for him. "I was able to step outside myself to do this record, to become a performer of the songs rather than the writer. That's the main difference—every song was performed. I wrote the songs describing the situations and then I became an extension of those situations and I performed them.

"It's like being an actor and writing the script for myself as opposed to a personal expression. There's obviously a lot of personal expression in there, but it comes in a different form, which makes it seem much more explicit and much more direct. All these people, they're all in there. That's why there's so much talking on the record. It's all the things that I hear people saying.

"I've been listening to this album for about two years and I'm not tired of it, it's a good friend of mine. In some respects I feel like it has more life than anything I've ever done. It's not the kind of life that jumps up and down and makes everybody smile. It's another kind of life—there's a feeling in it that's really strong.

"I don't think *Tonight's the Night* is a friendly album. It's real, that's all. Either you'll want to hear it or you won't. A lot of records don't even make you think that much. Then after that it will take you somewhere if you want to listen to it. I'm really proud of it. It's there for me. You've got to listen to it at night when it was done. Put on the Doobie Brothers in the morning. They can handle it at 11 a.m. But not this album. It's custom-made for night time."

While *Tonight's the Night* was taking shape for Neil, he continued to perform and record other albums. In 1974 he had joined in for the Crosby, Stills, Nash and Young tour that resulted in a retrospective album, *So Far*, which the group released in June of 1974. A month later Neil's solo, *On the Beach*, came out, to mostly rave reviews.

"Walk On" is the first song on *On the Beach*. It's fantastic, somewhat different from many of Neil's songs, and reappears again in his *Decade* album, on which he comments about it: "My own defensive reaction to criticisms of *Tonight's the Night* and the seemingly endless flow of money coming my way from you people out there." He opens the song with the line, *"I hear some people been talkin' me down / Bring up my name, pass it 'round / They don't mention the happy times / They do their thing, I do mine."* But it is also "a succinct rejection of Sixties fantasies," according to *Rolling Stone* reviewer Stephen Holden (September 26, 1974). The rejection revolves around the flat though somewhat bitter statement and refrain: *"Sooner or later it all gets real / Walk on."*

And that is more or less what you do in this album, walk on. Without actually being named, Charles Manson, Patricia Hearst, and Richard Nixon appear as symbols of the upheaval and social dislocation of the early 1970s. The album is like a guided tour through much of the insanity of this period. "Revolution Blues" and "Ambulance Blues" are the two songs in which Young "has dared what no other major white rock artist (except John Lennon) has—to embrace, expose and perhaps help purge the collective paranoia and guilt of an insane society, acting it out without apology or explanation," wrote Holden. "Since his days with Buffalo Springfield, the shifts in Neil Young's preoccupations have presented a barometer of a generation's attitudes toward itself, reflecting the dissolution of political idealism and, beyond that, the end of the romance of youth itself," Holden wrote. "Walk On," "Revolution Blues" and "Ambulance Blues" certainly support what Holden had to say.

"Whereas Bob Dylan's music formed the aesthetic spearhead of generational rage and moral fervor in the mid-Sixties, Young's subsequently expressed, with equal credibility, the accompanying guilt, self-doubt and paranoia, especially in its obsession with time and age," Holden commented.

Holden felt *On the Beach* was Young's best album since *After the Gold Rush*, and that its spare musicality and hard-edged sound was a contributing factor to its greatness, particularly "since the album poses aesthetic and political questions too serious to be treated prettily."

Ken Emerson in the *Village Voice* (August 22, 1974) felt that the music was the basic problem of *On the Beach*: "Doubtless its weakness is meant to mirror Young's subject matter—this *is* an album about debility. But the crude and rudimentary production, the simplistic musicianship, and the droning, flaccid tunes (most of which drag on far too long) run afoul of the imitative fallacy. The effect is appropriate but deadening."

The 9-minute cut "Ambulance Blues" closes the album. To Holden, it was "the tour de force of Young's recording career"; an arguable statement to many. In "Ambulance Blues," Neil sang at least an octave lower than he normally does, and the music was nice. Neil played acoustic guitar and harmonica and was backed by the incredible Doug Kershaw on fiddle. Holden saw "Ambulance Blues" as a summary of Neil's entire musical and political past, beginning with the idealism of "the old folky days," then impressionistically evoking specific social traumas, among them Watergate and the Hearst saga. ("*I saw today in the entertainment section / There's room at the top for private detection / To Mom and Dad this just doesn't matter / But it's either that or pay off the kidnappers.*")

Neil addresses us with a populist truism which he repeats in a voice that quietly spits in our faces: "*You're all just pissin' in the wind.*" The last verse

alludes to Nixon as both symptom and cause of a predicament that is frightening beyond comprehension:

"*I never knew a man could tell so many lies / He had a different story for every set of eyes / How can he remember who he's talkin' to / 'Cause I know it ain't me and I hope it isn't you.*"

"In its appeal to a post-revolutionary, post-psychedelic generation of young Americans, 'Ambulance Blues' stands as an epic lamentation, as irrefutable a piece of song-poetry as Paul Simon's 'American Tune' and Jackson Browne's 'For Everyman.' I could not imagine anyone but Young singing it," Holden analyzed.

Holden concludes his review of *On the Beach* with this statement: "On *the Beach* is one of the most despairing albums of the decade, a bitter testament from one who has come through the fire and gone back into it."

Bud Scoppa surveyed Neil's work up to *On the Beach* and concluded, in his *New Musical Express* article: "Young's first three albums—*Neil Young, Nowhere* and *After the Gold Rush*—have the irresistible power of beauty; his three most recent—*Time, Beach, Tonight* (I'm discounting the shallow and transitional *Harvest*)—have the grating power of deep anxiety. As a body of work, these albums display consistent eloquence, passion, and unflinching internal courage. *The man takes big chances*—he risks as much as any artist I can think of. Young's bravery works in support of his vision, fundamentally dark, bitter, and troubled, but always candidly, remarkably human. To use his own expression, Neil Young is really real."

Alvan Meyerowitz. San Francisco, 1975.

Richard McCaffree. S.N.A.C.K. Benefit, San Francisco, 1975   Chuck Krall

SHOP № 0007
Neil Faces the Sunny Days

Zuma, Neil's next album, came out at the end of 1975. It is his "daytime" album. He alluded to this album in his *New Musical Express* interview with Scoppa. "We're gonna just do it in the morning. Early in the morning, when the sun's out. Sunny days . . . just . . . play.

"It'll probably take about a week or two, then I'll be done with that. But I been practicin' for six weeks. I feel great about it. It's Molina, Talbot, and Pancho San Pedro [Frank Sampedro]: two guitars, bass, and drums. It's fun for me because I'm playing all the guitar, and I haven't played guitar in a long time . . . so I been practicing. I'm having a great time—I can fly all over the place now."

It is significant that Neil is back on guitar in this album; he had practically given it up after Danny Whitten's death. While he was writing and planning the songs for *Zuma*, he and his Crazy Horse group were performing in smaller places, coming together to make up for what was gone and trying to make themselves stronger and continue. "Because we thought we had it with Danny Whitten—at least, I did. I thought that I had a combination of people that could be as effective as groups like the Rolling Stones had been . . . just for rhythm, which I'm really into. I haven't been playing rhythm for a while and that's why I haven't been playing my guitar: because without that behind me I won't play. I mean you can't get free enough. So I've had to play the rhythm myself, ever since Danny died. Now I have someone who can play rhythm guitar (Frank Sampedro), a good friend of mine."

Zuma took shape in Neil's mind before he had even recorded one song. He knew he wanted to include a lot of long instrumental guitar pieces, what he called "progressive . . . progresso supremo." And he was sure of some of the images he wanted to invoke. "It's about the Incas and the Aztecs. It takes on another personality. It's like being in another civilization. It's a lost sort of form, sort of a soul form that switches from history scene to history scene trying to find itself, man, in this maze."

But as is the case in all of Neil's music, *Zuma* is intensely and agonizingly personal. It was written and recorded at a time when he and Carrie Snodgress seemed doomed to failure as a couple. He appeared obsessed with this failure, relating it not only to himself but to the history of the world in general. Ironically, other rock stars were facing similar disastrous relationships: 1975 saw the demise of Bob and Sara Dylan in *Blood on the Tracks*; Paul Simon poured his broken heart out in *Still Crazy After All These Years*; we heard Willie Nelson's lament in *Red Headed Stranger*. But when *Zuma* hit in November, Paul Nelson of the *Village Voice* (November 24, 1975) was the first to single it out as Neil's finest record yet, and the best example of what he refers to as this new genre: "Now Neil Young takes us on a primal, near-tribal journey from the erogenous to the combat zone, and makes us feel every blow with an intensity that is almost homicidal."

Bud Scoppa, obviously a steady fan of Neil's, heaped praise on *Zuma* in his *Rolling Stone* review a few months later (January 15, 1976): "Neil Young's ninth solo album is by far the best album he's made; it's the most cohesive (but not the most obvious) concept album I've ever encountered; and despite its depths, *Zuma* is so listenable that it should become Young's first hit album since *Harvest*."

Both reviewers agreed that "Cortez the Killer" was the best song on the album. On the surface, it is a historic tale of the Spaniards conquering the Aztecs, but its deeper meaning is personal. Scoppa wrote: "Cortez is an extended narrative tale that packs equal wallop as a classic retelling of an American legend, a Lawrencian erotic dreamscape and Young's ultimate personal metaphor." Paul Nelson commented, "Its exquisite sexual imagery, its depiction of savaged innocence, and the surprising last verse in which Young and his lost love suddenly and incongruously appear make it finally more personal than panoramic."

"Cortez the Killer" is epic in length (7:29 minutes) and builds in intensity, with the beginning several minutes given over to Neil's brilliant guitar solo. The first verse evokes a powerful sexual image: "*He came dancing across the water / With his galleons and guns / Looking for the new world / and that palace in the sun.*" Riches and beauty abound in this world. "*On the shore lay Montezuma / with his coca leaves and pearls / In his halls he often wandered / with the secrets of the worlds.*" He is surrounded by his subjects in clothes of many colours, "*like the leaves around a tree.*" The women are nothing less than beautiful; the men straight and strong. They lived in peace and offer up their own lives to build a better world, "*so that others could go on.*" To this world comes the ravager: "*He came dancing across the water. Cortez, Cortez. What a killer.*"

Bud Scoppa provided this interpretation: "The secret of the album, indeed of Young's work in its entirety, is encapsulated in this confrontation: force and wisdom, innocence and aggression, love and death are the issues and the stakes. And the climax is inevitable, but not before Young succumbs for a single verse to a direct comment on the classic struggle: *"And I know she's living there / and she loves me to this day. / I still can't remember when / or how I lost my way."*

Paul Nelson looked at the conflict in much the same way and related "Cortez the Killer" to the rest of the album in his review: "If 'Cotez' lends to ravaged romance an air of universal sadness and timeless treachery which suggests that even in Eden there is no hope for a satisfactory love

affair, much of the rest of the album is the artist's furious reaction to that 'reality.'"

The first song, "Don't Cry No Tears," allows for no whining about the fact that *"old true love ain't too hard to see,"* and that no matter who's with her now and holding her tight, *"there's nothing I can say / to make him go away."*

Neil's guitar work that so stamps this album as truly brilliant first comes to play in "Danger Bird." This is a tortured song, with two verses vying for attention at the same time, Neil singing both of them in different voices and playing beautifully in between, weaving in and out, giving true meaning and depth to the complex lyrics. Commenting on what makes this album truly marvelous, Bud Scoppa gave full credit to the band and Neil's exceptional playing: "What finally causes the album to burst into greatness is the presence of Crazy Horse, which has finally found in rhythm guitarist Frank Sampedro an adequate replacement for Danny Whitten. Sampedro's majestic rhythm work urges Young to what is clearly the most powerful guitar playing he's ever recorded. His guitar lines snake through Sampedro's

Alvan Meyerowitz. Berkeley, 1975

chordings with the dangerous snap of exposed wires crossing. Young's solos throughout more than match the eloquence of his lyrics, transmitting anguish, violence, joy and longing. With Crazy Horse providing both firepower and stability, Young is at his best: boundlessly inventive and determinedly multileveled."

Paul Nelson had express the same sentiments in his review: "Young rips almost the whole of *Zuma* open with some of the most vulnerable, visceral, and evocative electric guitar playing I've ever heard. Dominating and truly agonized, it tears at the soul with even more insistence than the gripping vocals and lyrics—and seems to inspire Crazy Horse to new heights of poignant, violent rock 'n' roll."

Poignant and violent, eloquent and anguished, joyful and full of longing—so many conflicting emotions are expressed throughout *Zuma* that it really does evolve into a world complete into itself. "Danger Bird" is eerie and painful: *"The jailbird takes the raps / And he finds himself spread-eagled on the tracks / But the training that he learned will get him no-where fast."* Images such as *"his wings have turned to stone"* are backed by others like *"freedom's just a prison to me."* This harsh song is followed by the exquisite, soft ballad, "Pardon My Heart." The first half contains the anger, the fight, and the accusations found in a relationship going wrong. But it's sung as softly as if it were a love song of affirmation. *"(You brought it all on) / Oh, but it feels so wrong / (You brought it all on) / No No No I don't believe this song."* The second half, sung in the same softness, calls up all the feelings aroused in making up: *"Pardon my heart / if I showed that I cared / But I love you more than moments / We have or have not shared. . . . Oh, and it feels so good / (You brought it all on) / When love flows the way that it should. . . ."*

"Lookin' for a Love" reveals Neil once again as the ultimate romantic. It's delightful, sung in a talkative country-and-western style, in Neil's "lower" voice. In it, he's still looking for that quintessential lover: *"In her eyes I will discover / another reason why / I want to live and make the best of what I see."* Right out of the *True Romance* magazine is how he envisions finding her. *"Where the sun hits the water / and the mountains meet the sand / there's a beach that I walk along sometimes / And maybe there I'll meet her, / and we'll start to say 'hello' / and never stop to think of any other time."*

"Barstool Blues" reveals again Neil's anguish over his breakup with Carrie: *"I have seen you in the movies / and those magazines at night / I saw you on the barstool when / you held that glass so tight / And I saw you in my nightmares / but I'll see you in my dreams. / And I might live a thousand years / before I know what that means."*

He is angry in "Stupid Girl," expressing the pain over his lost love in cathartic anger. It's a terrific song, Neil singing a duet with himself, with his very low voice backed by his high-pitched one: *"You're just a stupid girl / you really got a lot to learn . . . You're such a beautiful fish / floppin' on the summer sand. / Lookin' for the wave you missed / when another is close at hand."* And he's still angry in "Drive Back," a hard-rock number that reflects this mood: *"Drive back to your old town / I wanna wake up with no-one around."*

Crosby, Stills and Nash join Young on the last song of the album, "Through My Sails"—haunting, beautifully harmonic, and multileveled in meaning. As in most true poetry, the listener comes away with more than one interpretation. Nelson saw the conflicts in "Through My Sails" as clearcut and as black-and-white as the album itself is: "It is obvious that some sort of emotional resolution has been reached here, but whether the artist ends with the optimism of a new beginning or suicide is not made clear. Lines like 'Still glaring from the city lights/Into paradise I soar' and 'Wind blowing through my sails/It feels like I'm gone' can be read either way." Nelson opted for the former interpretation—optimism—and hopes Young does, too. "He has come through brilliantly in 1975," concluded Nelson. "*Tonight's the Night* and *Zuma* are powerful, tangible evidence that things can't be all bad, even when they seem to be."

Bud Scoppa found "Through My Sails" purely positive. "In the brief final ballad, Young, soaring on wings that have 'turned to stone,' lands finally on a shoreline where he transforms his wings into sails and sings, '*Know me/Show me . . . /New things I'm knowin'.*' Then off he sails."

Most listeners would agree, or want to agree, that the album ends optimistically. Overall and throughout, affirmation rather than negativism prevails. While Neil still clings to images of birds and sails and women carrying him away to ultimate truths and happiness, he seems to have come to the realization that this is not the way life is and it has not left him bitter. "Apparently tempered gloom is the brightest this love- and death-haunted epileptic genius can manage these days," writes Scoppa. "For Young, this insight holds both terror and liberation."

In between *Zuma* and his highly acclaimed *American Stars 'n Bars*, Neil got together with old friend Steve Stills and released *Long May You Run* in September 1976. It is truly an egalitarian collaboration, with five songs by Neil and four by Steve, backed by the Stills-Young Band, which included, besides the two leads, Joe Lala, Jerry Aiello, George "Chocolate" Perry, and Joe Vitale. All the songs were written in 1976, and the entire album was recorded in Miami. Most of the five songs by Neil seem to have been written while he was in Miami, because they summon up images of water, sand, sun, sails and sensuous tropicalia, as well as "all the blue-haired ladies and the wheelchairs."

The title song from the album, "Long May You Run," was "written for my first car and my last lady," Neil tells us on *Decade*. "As Dylan says, 'Now that the past is gone.'"

"Midnight on the Bay" is nice and easy, with acoustic guitar and bongos. It captures and evokes the sensuous pleasure and ease felt after a long day in the sun on a sailboat bathed by the ocean breeze: "*It's midnight on the bay/and lights are shinin'/and the sailboats sway./And that cool ocean breeze/blowin' down through the Keys./I think I'll call it a day./Oh, midnight on the bay,/sure feels good to me.*" To top it all off, whether fantasy or fact, up comes a lovely maiden out of the blue who'd like to spend some time: "*What's this I see,/someone comin',/walkin' right up to me./She tells me I know your name/and if it's all the same/I'd like to spend some time./And midnight on the bay/sure feels good to me.*"

"Ocean Girl" concludes Side One in an upbeat, light rock style backed with bongos. *"In the jungle land with the sea and the sand / can I meet you there? / We'll be drinkin' bananas from the long tall glasses / in the open air."*

Neil opens Side Two with "Let It Shine," a good-ole-time-religion song, which he sings in his twangy country voice. An electric lead is followed by nice country rock and harmonica with terrific guitar work in between verses.

"Fountainebleau" evokes Miami also, the Miami that scared Neil because "I stayed there once and I almost fit." But it is funny, too: *"Who put the palm over my blond? / Who put all the tar on the morning sand? / Who took everything from where it once was / and put it where it last was seen? / Fontainebleau, they painted it green. / Fontainebleau, for the well-to-do, / at the Fontainebleau."*

The songs on Long May You Run are just "nice." They are like easy pieces in between the hard ones. It is almost as if Neil were on a brief vacation and threw together some pretty lyrics and melodies for a friend, to preserve a special time they shared together. It is quite a jump from this album to American Stars 'n Bars.

Released in June of 1977, American Stars 'n Bars "is a good introduction to Young," wrote John Rockwell in his rave review in The New York Times (June 19, 1977), in that "unlike his recent solo albums, it blends several different kinds of his music." Rockwell thought On the Beach, Tonight's the Night, and Zuma were all "great records," but that on them Neil found himself "lost in a brooding, private world." He realized that all three albums were intentionally personal ones and, because of that, "almost defiant in their refusal to reach out to a wide audience." And while he didn't feel American Stars 'n Bars was necessarily going to sell millions, Rockwell noted that Side One "finds Young working in a lighter, brighter idiom than in the past."

Rockwell continued: "Recorded in April of this year [1977] and featuring highly audible, pervasive vocals by Linda Ronstadt and Nicolette Larson (an excellent Los Angeles session singer), this is a collection of country-and-Westernish tunes that emerge almost as trios rather than as solos with back-up vocal accompaniment. Compared to the great, tortured Neil Young epics, these may seem superficial at first. But soon enough one realizes that there is a seriousness here, and Young's unique style lends them an inescapable resonance."

In addition to harmonies by Ronstadt and Larson, the five songs on Side One feature guitarist Frank Sampedro, bassist Billy Talbot, drummer Ralph Molina (the Crazy Horse trio), as well as Ben Keith on steel guitar and Carole Mayedo on violin.

For Ken Tucker, writing in Circus Magazine, "it is the hard country music of Side One that makes the album both aesthetically successful and the artist's most commercially pleasing collection since the sore thumb of his career, *Harvest* . . . . Throughout the first side, Young is just another guy on a barstool, yowling to be heard and playing lead guitar as if he were riding out a mean, melancholy drunk."

Ken Marks, in his review in *The Berkshire Sampler* on July 3, 1977, concurred: "The feeling created is that of an easy-going but powerful roadhouse bar band who've been partying along with the patrons. It's the most consistently lighthearted sound Young has ever captured and one which offers an ironic counterpoint to many of the lyrics."

Marks continued: "The texture of the opening track, 'The Old Country Waltz,' sets the tone for the side. Crazy Horse proceeds methodically. Young strums an acoustic, his reedy voice and the fiddle approximate the proper pitch, the steel guitar and women's voices add sweetness and consistency to the mixture without ever threatening to turn it to mush."

Neil sang *"Well I loved . . . and I lost . . . and I cried. / The day that the two of us died. / Ain't got no excuses . . . / I just want to ride while the band plays the old country waltz"*; Marks noted Young "feels a little misty and will indulge in some pure nostalgia for a lost love rather than fight the sentiment."

"'Saddle Up the Palomino' begins with a giggling Ronstadt," wrote Marks, "as good an indication as any of the relative playfulness of this disc. This song about split-level frontier adultery contains the record's funniest line: 'It's a cold bowl of chili when love lets you down / But it's the neighbor's wife I'm after.'"

Marks though "Hey Babe" was: "positively bouncy for a Neil Young song. Here, Young's dreams for a perfect love come smack up against his all too acute sense of reality: 'I know that all things pass / Let's try and make this last.'"

"Hold Back the Tears" and "Bite the Bullet" exalt in what Tucker described as "the strength to be drawn from a strident, often violently imposed stoicism." Young whines and cries movingly to an old friend: *"Hold back the tears / And keep on tryin' / Just around the next corner may be waiting / Your true love."* Still he manages to be a bit tongue-in-cheek in this one: *"And single life / Really has its fine points / Like friends to help you out / When things go wrong."* Whether giving or receiving the advice and helpful suggestion in this song, Young still reveals himself as the eternal optimist, even though this outlook is fraught with frustrations. In "Bite the Bullet" we find Young moving right from the romantic to the sexual side of love, strapping on his electric guitar for this number. "It's a driving, confident, insistent track that repeats the title after almost every line, Ronstadt soaring on top," wrote Marks.

For Tucker, "Bite the Bullet" was the toughest on the album, and the one in which both melody and lyrics match perfectly. "Instead of his usual oblique approach to his amorous desires—for all the rocker in him, this art-

Neal Preston/Mirage. Last Waltz tour, 1977

ist is nearly always chastely polite and romantic when he wants to impress or seduce a woman (something he doesn't want to do very often, however)—Young here celebrates a 'walking love machine' and says he'd 'like to make her scream.' This passion is rendered by the slamming melody, in which the phrase 'bite the bullet' is the singer's way of keeping himself psyched up and persistent in the conquest of this amazing desired one (who is, by the way, a 'barhall queen' in Charlotte, North Carolina)."

While Side One of *American Stars 'n Bars* includes only songs written and recorded in 1977, Side Two includes some written and recorded as far back as 1974. And it is a totally different Neil Young on this side; it is the far more serious Neil that is revealed singing songs that soar and plunge and

peak as only his classics can. "Except for the jolly final number, the second side plunges right back into Young at his most intense," wrote John Rockwell. "The first song, recorded in November of 1974—Young reportedly has whole albums worth of unreleased material—is called 'Star of Bethlehem,' and features Emmylou Harris in another of her marvelously haunting backup roles. In a song called 'Cortez the Killer' on the *Zuma* album, Young painted a whole hisotircal fresco and then magically transformed it into a metaphor for personal love. In 'Star of Bethlehem' he sets an intimate scene and then projects it outward into Christian imagery. Either way, both songs capture Young at his finest."

Ken Marks offered this interpretation: "'Star of Bethlehem'... packs a broad poetic sampling of Young's philosophy. We're at the mercy of our illusions, he tells us, destined to relive and reaffirm the fallacy of our hopes and beliefs time after time. The comparison at the end of a memory-inducing bare light bulb in a hallway to the symbol of the title is as moving as—I suspect—it is sacrilegious." The lyrics Marks referred to are: *"Yet still a light is shining/From that lamp on down the hall./Maybe the star of Bethlehem/Wasn't a star at all."*

The next song is truly remarkable and pretty. Almost like a confession, a "fireside chat," Neil recorded "The Will to Love" in his own home in

front of an audibly crackling fireplace on a simple, 2-track Sony cassette recorder in May of 1976. As John Rockwell saw it, "This is as exact a statement as one could find of his despair, loneliness and eternal romanticism."

Neil began and ended with the phrase: *"It has often been my dream/to live with one who wasn't there."* The impossible dream? And his symbol throughout for his own indomitable will to love is that of *"an ocean fish who swam upstream/Through nets, big hooks, and hungry bears."* This extraordinary will is something he can never lose, and it is both a blessing and a curse: *"Cool running love keeps cleansing me./It keeps my gills from getting dry/*

But it distorts things in my eye / Sometimes I see what isn't there / Like my true lover and I care."

"'Like a Hurricane' from November of 1975 offers Young the tortured electric guitarist at his most impassioned," wrote Rockwell. Dennis Petticoffer, in his column "Hot Wax," felt Young "blows the listener away" in this song, "with his finest jam since 'Down by the River,' a churning storm of electric music. Superlative tracks such as this one contribute to make *American Stars 'n Bars* the most aggressive and exuberant Neil Young album to date."

Marks went even further: "'Like a Hurricane' contains the inspiration for the album's title and its raunchy cover art depicting a floor's-eye view of

Richard McCaffree. Santa Cruz, 1977

the universe. The stars represent the sought-after ideal, the bars, a more mundane reality. 'I'm getting blown away / To somewhere safer where the feeling stays / I want to love you / But I'm getting blown away.' There Young launches into the album's one long, bravado guitar break and it is a beauty. He plays as if with an exposed, raw, naked wire and gets off on the danger, teasing it, taming it, losing control and barely regaining it before the song ends."

Some of Neil's most beautiful, poetic images are contained in "Like a Hurricane," and Rockwell alluded to this song in his review of the album, when he wrote: "Young's metaphors reach innocently and incessantly to the heavens—in *American Stars 'n Bars* he sees a lover 'Dancing on the light from star to star,/Far across the moonbeams'—and partly as a result his poetic imagery attains a depth and simplicity that match some of the greatest American poetry."

That is indeed remarkably high praise from the nation's number-one contemporary music critic; but Neil Young deserves no less. For fully ten years he has produced what now amounts to volumes of poetic lyrics that can rightly be compared to "some of the greatest American poetry." His talent as a poet is matched equally by his musical genius.

To conclude this most recent masterwork, Neil Young offers us a gentle beauty, "Homegrown." With considerable thought given to just how to end *American Stars 'n Bars*, Neil chose a song that would let us go in a much lighter mood. Recorded in November of 1975, "Homegrown" is jolly and fun. "An electric gardening sing-along," is how Marks described it. "[It] closes the album without a trace of seriousness, and it's welcome."

"Sun comes up in the morning/And it shines that light around./One day without no warning/Things start jumpin' up from the ground./

Well homegrown's alright with me/Homegrown is the way it should be/Homegrown is a good thing/Plant that bell and let it ring!"/

American Stars 'n Bars really lit up the night for just about everyone when it came out. "Neil's got plenty to say on the new album—and oh, how he says it!" wrote Petticoffer. He observed that it "represents the culmination of Young's personal renaissance."

Ken Tucker noted, "The richness of its jaggedly precise music and nonchalantly sentimental/bizarre lyrics lift it away from the music that anyone else is making today. . . . *American Stars 'n Bars* is yet another step forward in Neil Young's musical evolution, one that is shaping up as possibly the most interesting and involving in rock & roll in the seventies."

As is the case in lives that come together and separate frequently over a period of years, Neil's former cohorts in the superstar world of rock 'n roll—Crosby, Stills and Nash—came out with their own album, simply titled *C S N*, within the same week as *American Stars 'n Bars*. Remarkably, this was the second album the threesome had produced as a group—their first had been in 1969, *Crosby, Stills and Nash*.

Individually and collectively, Crosby, Stills, Nash and Young have managed to produce a remarkable total of 30 albums (32 actual LP's), including a few "greatest hits" collections, their two new albums, and Neil's retrospective, *Decade*.

"The reason for the large number of discs is that these are all talented men and their various couplings produce music that is both interesting and popular," wrote John Rockwell. "The reason for the variety of couplings is that they clash frequently, both artistically and personally. . . . Young is the real loner of the foursome, technically rawer and temperamentally isolated. He is also far and away the finest artist of the lot."

Rockwell, as well as several other critics, found C S N to be a weak album in general, mainly because of its "lack of energy." This reception was in total contrast to the way in which everyone was reacting to the now fully matured Neil Young. "Young's position as a solo artist is firmly established," affirmed Rockwell. "He may not be the hottest seller in popular music, nor has he yet won quite the degree of recognition that he deserves. But he is still about as individual, talented and touching a musical poet as American popular music has produced, worthy of comparison with Bob Dylan.

"Young surpasses not only Crosby, Stills and Nash, but indeed the vast majority of contemporary singer-songwriters on several grounds. His basic stance is clear, even if it is obscured by evocative ambiguities. Neil Young is the quintessential hippy-cowboy loner, a hopeless romantic struggling to build bridges out from himself to women and through them to cosmic archetypes of the past and of myth. He is a mystic of a very particular type, however, and that has limited his commercial appeal and perhaps, his artistic range. Not everyone can feel comfortable with a stoned California hippie lowlifer. . . . Yet that same hermetic self-indulgence protects him from a slicker self-consciousness that often undercuts the work of C S & N and the others. . . .

"Musically, too, Young stands aside from the Los Angeles folk-rock school that Crosby, Stills and Nash epitomize. Not for him the smooth harmonies and precise, well-tuned, tasteful instrumentation of his peers. The instrumental sound favored by his band, Crazy Horse, is solid and monolithic, with leaden drumming and blocky guitar chords lent an unmistakable flavor by their slightly sour tuning. Young's voice, a quavery, poignant tenor, is far from technically ideal, yet its rawness is itself a metaphor for vulnerability. In sum, Young is an artist who has found a perfect outlet for his limitations and his vision in his highly personalized rock-and-roll—which is itself an art form made for the propagation of passionate, technically simple art. . . .

"One imagines many people will buy and enjoy the new C S N disc and the trio's live shows. Perhaps some or all of the threesome will collaborate with Young in the future, and worthy music may result. But of the four, Neil Young is the artist. One hopes that long-delayed three-disc album of his great songs of the past decade (due out in the fall of 1977) will inspire the critical reassessment that will establish him rightfully in the patheon of post-war American popular art," Rockwell concluded.

The 3-disc album referred to by Rockwell, *Decade*, was finally released in the late fall of 1977 and will undoubtedly establish Neil as one of the major contributors to popular art in contemporary America. The album includes the songs most people consider his greatest: the Crosby, Stills, Nash and Young tunes "Helpless" and "Ohio;" the Buffalo Springfield tunes "Mr. Soul," "I Am a Child," "Broken Arrow," "Burned," "Expecting to Fly" and the previously unreleased "Down to the Wire;" four of his own previously unreleased tunes—"Deep Forbidden Lake," "Love Is a Rose," "Winterlong," and "Campaigner;" his early hit single, "Sugar Mountain;" and many more. It is a joy to listen to, and sure to be written and talked about in the years ahead as a major retrospective not only of Neil's music, but also of the state of the music scene over the last ten years.

Neil's words and music have always mirrored the times—politically, socially, and personally. After listening to him closely over a 10-year period, we get the feeling that this extraordinarily private man has, after all, told us a great deal about himself.

Tall, thin and gangly, he has never been in the best of health. His brooding withdrawals from the public have been triggered not only by his need to continually redefine his own vision of himself as a superstar, but by critical health problems as well. Throughout most of 1971, he was bedridden with a back ailment that made it impossible for him to play the electric guitar. In 1975 he was operated on for removal of nodes on his vocal cords. And he has suffered occasionally over the years from epilepsy and diabetes.

On the subject of drugs, Neil Young is quite clear. While he has never been incapacitated by drugs, he readily admits to the use of alcohol and softer drugs, particularly when writing and recording. They help open the avenues to his creative process, along with mystical insights that let him know when to record. "Drugs are not my life; that's for sure. I'm a survivor," he told John Rockwell, *The New York Times*, November 27, 1977. "Now, the avenue may be there anyway, and maybe someone else could go down that avenue without that, and maybe I could if I had to. But it affected my writing, no doubt about it."

About his lighter side, we know of his deep love and respect for nature. Images of birds, sailboats, water, and the Western scene provide a lyrical respite from heavier ones of night and death in his songs. We can sense that he is often blunt and to the point, independent and tough-minded, but that he is innately fair in his dealings with people, and that his wry sense of humor softens his harder edge.

He is obviously a loner, but maintains very close family ties, even though we know from his songs that he suffered from a terribly unhappy childhood. His strong need for privacy has made it necessary for him to keep very tight control over every aspect of his life. Friends and the people who work with Neil—particularly manager and long-time friend Elliot Roberts—obviously respect his privacy and help protect him from unwanted exposure to the public and press. Of course, his reclusiveness only enhances his elusive, dark, moody, mysterious and romantic image.

Over the years, Neil's fans have come to know him best as one of the true great romantics of our time. He is the undaunted searcher for the one true love, the heart of gold. He has been hurt and disappointed by love; he has gone through much anguish and bitterness because of it. And although he never publicly discussed his on-again-off-again relationship with Carrie Snodgress, it is evident that their final split brought him a great deal of pain.

Carrie herself tends to view their separation in a lighter vein, as is evident in the statement she made to The New York Times on August 19, 1977. "Neil and I had a good six years together. We never bothered with a marriage license; I wanted him to think of me as somebody *different*, not a wife. When we had problems, we had to *talk* to each other about them, not to a court. And no judge tells Neil that he can visit his son on weekends only. Oddly enough, everything worked out just as we had planned from the beginning. We always said that when one of us wanted to end it, we would end it. We never had bad times, and we still see one another."

Which one made the final decision to end it? Carrie doesn't say, and neither does Neil. But it is definitely over, and she is back in the movie business after a 6-year hiatus.

"I understand how things work in Hollywood," Carrie told the interviewer, looking back over the difficulty she had re-entering her profession. "The industry wants its actors to *work*, to present themselves to the public over and over, so that people will be curious to see them in any movie, no matter how good or bad it is. They invested a lot of energy in making me a star, but then I dropped out and that didn't make the industry smile. So when I decided to come back, they didn't trust me. Rock-and-roll carries a heavy stigma out there, and they didn't want to fool around with any dropout on a drug-induced, back-to-nature trip. . . . I'm very grateful to Frank Yablans for giving me this chance. [She can be seen in the movie The Fury.] He knew that if I did what I did before, I could still do it. If you've got a talent, you don't *lose* it. It's just a matter of time for people to see that I was sincere in my reasons for dropping out, that it wasn't because I was incapable of handling success." She explained that she had just found it impossible to handle a career, a baby, and Neil all at the same time. "Now the industry needs to see that I'm walking straight, looking good, and still smiling."

So is Neil, it seems. He currently has custody of their 5-year-old son, Zeke. And with the release in 1977 of American Stars 'n Bars and Decade, he is even more firmly established as one of rock's superstars of the 1970s and as one of its most articulate, creative, and prolific artists. He's already had a remarkable influence on the "new wave" of music coming out in the late 1970s. As John Rockwell wrote in his glowing review of *Decade* in *The New York Times*, November 27, 1977: "His primitivism anticipated the renewal of angry energy that characterizes today's punk rockers; it's no accident, for all their vast differences, that Johnny Rotten of the Sex Pistols counts Neil Young as one of his favorite musicians."

In the spring of 1978, while *Decade* is still on the charts, Neil plans to release a new album he recorded in Nashville and then go on tour. In the meantime, he will continue his restless traveling. According to Rockwell, Neil reports that "in the last three years he's never spent more than eight weeks in any one place." After he finishes building a 75-foot schooner in Florida—complete with a 16-track studio—he plans to sail around the world.

As this decade draws to a close, it does so with none of the foreboding that accompanied the end of the 1960s. Rather, a sense of optimism prevails, and Neil's fans can justifiably count themselves among the most optimistic of all. As Neil told John Rockwell, "You just keep on going. Now, when I get into something, I say, 'You know, I'm just on my own course here. I'm liable to be gone at any time. So whatever we do, every moment is *it*, forever. There's no build; we're already at the top.'"

SHOP № 0008
Discography

*not by Neil Young

Solo Albums [Reprise]

Neil Young
RS 6317, January 1969

The Loner
If I Could Have Her Tonight
The Old Laughing Lady
I've Been Waiting for You
*String Quartet
Here We Are in the Years
What Did You Do to My Life
*I've Loved Her So Long
The Last Trip to Tulsa

Everybody Knows This Is Nowhere
RS 6349, May 1969

Cinnamon Girl
Everybody Knows This Is Nowhere
Round & Round (It Won't Be Long)
Down by the River
The Losing End (When You're On)
Running Dry (Requiem for the Rockets)
Cowgirl in the Sand

After the Gold Rush
RS 6383, August 1970

Tell Me Why
After the Gold Rush
Only Love Can Break Your Heart
Southern Man
Till the Morning Comes
*Oh, Lonesome Me
Don't Let It Bring You Down
Birds
When You Dance You Really Can Love
I Believe in You
Cripple Creek Ferry

Harvest
MS 2032, February 1972

Out on the Weekend
Harvest
A Man Needs a Maid
Heart of Gold
Are You Ready for the Country
Old Man
There's a World
Alabama
The Needle and the Damage Done
Words (Between the Lines of Age)

Journey Through the Past
2XS 6480, November 1972

*For What It's Worth
Mr. Soul
*Rock and Roll Woman
*Find the Cost of Freedom
Ohio
Southern Man
Are You Ready for the Country
*Let Me Call You Sweetheart
Alabama
Words
Relativity Invitation
*Handel's Messiah
*The King of Kings Theme
Soldier
*Let's Go Away for Awhile

123

Robert Ellis

Time Fades Away
MS 2151, October 1973

Time Fades Away
Journey Thru the Past
Yonder Stands the Sinner
L.A.
Love in Mind
Don't Be Denied
The Bridge
Last Dance

On the Beach
R 2180, July 1974

Walk On
See the Sky About to Rain
Revolution Blues
For the Turnstiles
Vampire Blues
On the Beach
Motion Pictures
Ambulance Blues

Tonight's the Night
MS 2221, July 1975

Tonight's the Night
Speakin' Out
World on a String
Borrowed Tune
*Come on Baby Let's Go Downtown
Mellow My Mind
Roll Another Number (For the Road)
Albuquerque
New Mama
Lookout Joe
Tired Eyes
Tonight's the Night—Part II

Zuma
MS 2242, November 1975

Don't Cry No Tears
Danger Bird
Pardon My Heart
Lookin' for a Love
Barstool Blues
Stupid Girl
Drive Back
Cortez the Killer
Through My Sails

American Stars 'n Bars
MSK 2261, June 1977

The Old Country Waltz
Saddle up the Palomino
Hey Babe
Hold Back the Tears
Bite the Bullet
Star of Bethlehem
Will to Love
Like a Hurricane
Homegrown

Decade
3RS 2257, October 1977

Down to the Wire
Burned
Mr. Soul
Broken Arrow
Expecting to Fly
Sugar Mountain
I Am a Child
The Loner
The Old Laughing Lady
Cinnamon Girl
Down by the River
Cowgirl in the Sand
I Believe in You
After the Gold Rush
Southern Man
Helpless
Ohio
Soldier
Old Man
A Man Needs a Maid
Harvest
Heart of Gold
Star of Bethlehem
The Needle and the Damage Done
Tonight's the Night (Part I)
Tired Eyes
Walk On
For the Turnstiles
Winterlong
Deep Forbidden Lake
Like a Hurricane
Love Is a Rose
Cortez the Killer
Campaigner
Long May You Run

With Buffalo Springfield [Atco]

Buffalo Springfield
SD 33-200, February 1967

*For What It's Worth
*Go and Say Goodbye
*Sit Down, I Think I Love You
 Nowadays Clancy Can't Even Sing
*Hot Dusty Roads
*Everybody's Wrong
 Flying on the Ground Is Wrong
 Burned
 Do I Have to Come Right Out and Say It
*Leave
 Out of My Mind
*Pay the Price

Buffalo Springfield Again
SD 33-226, December 1967

 Mr. Soul
*A Child's Claim to Fame
*Everydays
 Expecting to Fly
*Bluebird
*Hung Upside Down
*Sad Memory
*Good Time Boy
*Rock 'n Roll Woman
 Broken Arrow

Last Time Around
SD 33-256, August 1968

 On the Way Home
 It's So Hard to Wait
*Pretty Girl Why
*Four Days Gone
*Carefree Country Day
*Special Care
*The Hours of Not Quite Rain
*Questions
 I Am a Child
*Merry-Go-Round
*Uno Mundo
*Kind Woman

Retrospective/The Best of the Buffalo Springfield
SD 33-283, January 1969

*For What It's Worth
 Mr. Soul
*Sit Down, I Think I Love You
*Kind Woman
*Bluebird
 On the Way Home
 Nowadays Clancy Can't Even Sing
 Broken Arrow
*Rock 'n Roll Woman
 I Am a Child
*Go and Say Goodbye
 Expecting to Fly

With Crosby, Stills, Nash and Young [Atlantic]

Déjà Vu
SD 7200, March 1970

*Carry On
*Teach Your Children
*Almost Cut My Hair
 Helpless
*Woodstock
*Déjà Vu
*Our House
*4 & 20
 Country Girl
  a. Whiskey Boot Hill
  b. Down, Down, Down
  c. "Country Girl" (I Think You're Pretty)
 Everybody I Love You

4 Way Street
SD 2-902, April 1971

*Suite: Judy Blue Eyes
 On the Way Home
*Teach Your Children
*Triad
*The Lee Shore
*Chicago
*Right Between the Eyes
 Cowgirl in the Sand
 Don't Let It Bring You Down
*49 Bye Byes/America's Children

*Love the One You're With
*Pre-Road Downs
*Long Time Gone
　Southern Man
　Ohio
*Carry On
*Find the Cost of Freedom

With the Stills-Young Band [*Reprise*]

Long May You Run
MS 2253, *September 1976*

　Long May You Run
*Make Love to You
　Midnight on the Bay
*Black Coral
　Ocean Girl
　Let It Shine
*12/8 Blues (All the Same)
　Fontainebleau
*Guardian Angel